Time-Honored
Norwegian
Recipes

Adapted to the
American
Kitchen

D0931741

Penfield
Press

Time-Honored
Norwegian
Recipes

Adapted to the American Kitchen

by Erna Oleson Xan and Sigrid Marstrander

Photographs by Dean Madden, Darrell Henning,
Joan Liffring-Zug, and Willis Wangsness.
Graphic design by Esther Feske and Judy Waterman.
Edited by John Zug.

This coffee set was a wedding gift to Sigrid and Henning Marstrander. It was created by her husband's cousin, a jeweler and artist, in hand-hammered sterling silver. The set is unique. Details from the Cathedral of Trondheim are depicted on the set. The lid of the coffee pot represents a bishop's hat.

Publisher's note: When he read *Wisconsin My Home,* Dr. Marion Nelson, director of Vesterheim, thought Erna Oleson Xan's writing style wonderful. He contacted her at her home in Birmingham, Alabama to see if she would compile a special cookbook for the museum. Mrs. Xan accepted the offer and requested that her good friend Sigrid Marstrander, a wonderful Norwegian cook, participate, too. This book is the result of their friendship and collaboration.

It was our pleasure to meet Mrs. Xan when she was living in Tallahassee, Florida with her daughter and son-in-law, Tom and Dixie Bullock. When we called Mrs. Marstrander, she said, "Next time. My oriental rugs are at the cleaners and everything is out of place." Unfortunately, there was no next time. Both authors lived into their 90s, good and graceful lives.—Joan Liffring-Zug.

You are invited to keep in contact with Norway in America through your membership in Vesterheim. Send for information, or begin your membership by sending $10 to Vesterheim, 502 West Water Street, Decorah, Iowa 52101 (1990 dues for Associate Member).

Front cover: Dane Thomas Bahr and Jon Anders Bahr, sons of LeAnn and Stephen Bahr of Maple Grove, Minnesota are shown in the Gudbrandsdalen House at Vesterheim, the Norwegian-American Museum. They are under a Christmas mobile of straw, called a Uhro. The coverlet at right is a type hung during festivals as a room decoration.

Back cover: Norma Wangsness of Decorah, Iowa, an accomplished rosemaler, poses in her Telemark bunad (costume). The cotton embroidery on the linen blouse and the wool embroidery on the loom-woven wool of the dress was done by Norma's mother, Christine Anderson, when she was 80 years old. At age 85, Mrs. Anderson embroidered the jacket.

Norma is noted for her costumed dolls wearing Norwegian bunads. Every year they decorate one of the Christmas trees at Vesterheim, the Norwegian-American Museum. Norma has degrees as a photographic craftsman and specialist from the Professional Photographers of America, Inc. She helps with many Vesterheim projects, including the photographs of people and their costumes in this book.

Background in the photograph is the Haugan House (circa 1859), part of the open-air museum (Friluft) at Vesterheim. Photograph by Willis Wangsness, Norma's husband.

© 1990, Norwegian-American Museum, Decorah, Iowa. All rights reserved. Printed in the United States of America. A revised edition of *Time-Honored Norwegian Recipes,* © 1974, Norwegian-American Museum.

Library of Congress catalog
number 90-60677
ISBN 0-941016-76-5

Contents

"The Best Cook in the World"   6

The Story of Sigrid   7

The Girl from Wisconsin   9

Time-Honored Notes   13

Soups and Porridges   14

Fish and Meat   18

Vegetables   25

Breads and Pancakes   30

Cakes, Cookies, and Desserts   35

Apple Pie in Norway   44

From the Vesterheim Collection   46

Costumes and Scenics in Color   49

Photographs of Norway   52

Norway in America   54

The Wedding in Norway   65

Fish in Norway   67

Christmas in Norway   67

Trondheim Cathedral   71

Tone: The Girl from Norway   72

Grandma Was Frugal   77

How I Wrote Wisconsin My Home   82

Food Preparation in Norway   90

Summertime in Norway   93

Making Bread and Butter   98

Mother's Greatest Fame   100

Meats, Potatoes, Berries, Nuts   103

Baking for Weddings   105

We Didn't Drink Milk   106

The Old Ironstone Platter   107

Child Helpers; and other Observations   108

The Aprons of Vesterheim   113

Embroidery by Grace Rikansrud   117

Jewelry and Silver at Vesterheim   118

1896 Photographs of Norway   120

Dayton House   126

'The Best Cook in the World'

It was Henning and John who made Sigrid and me what we are as cooks. Henning told people that his wife was the best cook in the world. My John almost never got up from the table without saying, "This was the best meal I ever ate." Of course, day by day, both Sigrid and I outdid ourselves, for praise is heady stuff to the cook.

Acknowledgments

In writing this book, Sigrid and I want to thank our children, the "green leaves and fruit" of our lives, for their love and support. Without them we would be lone trees in a winter field.

Sigrid has her daughter-in-law Jeanette Marstrander, and grandson Jon Rolf, an "A" student at the University of Alabama. We both claim as "sister" our cherished friend Nellie Cassidy, who has "heard" the book from cover to cover.

My family is daughter Dixie and her husband Thomas Bullock, and grandchildren Kathryn and Scott Ellis, school music teachers in Milledgeville, Georgia.

Sigrid's delicious Norwegian recipes came out of very old cookbooks which she carried around the world, making a home for her husband Henning and son Jan.

As for help in writing the stories, I leaned on my two lifetime champions. First is Dixie, who started me into story-telling when she was about three. Pounding my knees with her small fists, she would demand, "Not wead. *TELL!*" This did not mean that she was rejecting "The Three Bears" or "Chicken Little." But the enchantment of her mother's daily serial, "Brutus Beetle and the Walnut Trailer," or "Angleworm School," was a greater delight, because she could *help make it up!* Before she was five, I was selling children's stories.

My other literary comrade was my sister, Henrietta Bear. We were like twins, inseparable until I finished high school. Fascinated with words, she had a newspaper column called "The King's English," and sold magazine articles. We wove into each other's thoughts like the warp and the woof of a garment. In this present book, we worked by long distance telephone, or face-to-face. She brought up many a happy memory.

All would be for naught but for Marion Nelson, Director of the Norwegian-American Museum, Decorah, Iowa, who asked me to do the first edition of this book. He consented for Sigrid Marstrander to help me, and I would have had a hard time without her.

Erna Oleson Xan

The Story of Sigrid

By Erna Oleson Xan

Sigrid Guttormson Marstrander, destined for a most adventuresome life, was perfectly programmed for it by nature. She was healthy, intrepid, attractive, endearing, and always up to something exciting. She was what she was, to be what she became.

Born in Trondheim, Norway, February 3, 1891, she was brought up by her mother's elder sister, Ida Evenson, whose husband was a furrier, and who thought nothing was too good for their little girl. In high school Sigrid had some studies that were to affect her entire life. One was a year of art under an excellent teacher. Another was the study of languages. She learned to speak Norwegian, Swedish, Danish, German, English and a little French.

The city was the home of the renowned Trondheim Technical Institute, which had a student body of six hundred boys. One night while Sigrid was out skiing with one of them, he fell and broke his arm.

At that, he began to wail, "Professor Vogt! My *drawings!*"

"What about them?" Sigrid asked.

"They are due tomorrow."

Sigrid said not to worry, she could help, and he turned in the drawings the next morning.

The Professor looked at them, and then at the boy with his arm in a sling. "You did all these," he asked, "with a broken arm?"

"No," the boy confessed, "a girl did them."

"Bring that girl to me."

So that is how Sigrid became assistant and cartographer to one of the greatest geologists of his day, Professor J.H.L. Vogt, head of the Geology Department of the Institute. Losing no time, he instructed Sigrid in map-drawing, micro-photography, and filing of rock specimens for the institute's museum. It became her duty to write names and dates on diplomas in fancy script. Soon she was illustrating his famous books, with his name on one side of the drawings, and hers on the other.

When he lectured, she was beside him at the blackboard, sketching what he was talking about, while behind his back, the boys flirted and made eyes at the pretty, young assistant.

Among these students was a doctor's son from Oslo who was majoring in mine safety. Of middle height, and with eyes that twinkled even when he wanted to look dignified, Henning Marstrander was too bashful even to glance at Sigrid in the halls.

One day, during a lecture, when she was deftly drawing with great earnestness at the board, Henning tilted a window-blind so that a beam of sunlight fell right on her face. After that, of course, the only decent thing to do was to seek her out, beg her pardon, and ask for a date. Uncle Evenson looked him over, and finally consented. They went together three years, until Henning graduated.

By now Professor Vogt was so dependent and grateful for Sigrid's work that he arranged for her to be decorated with "The Star of Nidaros." This was

7

Sigrid Marstrander. Photograph by
Darrell Henning.

for unusual service to the Institute. It had never before been given to a woman. The nine-pointed silver star with two crossed miner's hammers was wreathed in gold and suspended on a blue ribbon. For the momentous occasion, Sigrid piled her blonde hair high on her head and wore an ankle-length, royal-blue silk dress. After kneeling to be 'knighted' with a sword, she rose to be pinned with the medal.

Finishing the five-year course in 1917, Henning received both Master's and Doctor's degrees in Mining Engineering and Economic Geology. His dissertation, for which he also received "The Star of Nidaros," won praise in four nations.

One evening before the wedding, as they sat alone, he showed her his class ring with a globe of the world on it. "Sigrid," he said quietly, "I may be sent anywhere there's mine trouble on earth. Will you go with me?"

Placing her hand on the ring, she looked up at him tenderly and replied, "Yes, Henning, I will."

Their marriage was at Trondheim Cathedral where the kings of Norway are crowned. In this same church, Sigrid had been christened and confirmed and had attended services all her life, and now she was bidding it goodbye.

For thirty years she and Henning traveled to many countries by boat, train, car and plane, staying two to four years at a time. In her trunks, Sigrid packed her pillows, family pictures, and cookbooks containing recipes that are now in this *Time-Honored Norwegian Recipes* book.

Their son, Jan, was born in Norway, and became a good traveler. Before he was born, they spent two years in Spitzbergen, above the Arctic Circle, where it was black night from October to February. Sigrid saved her sanity by establishing clubs for the miners' wives and schools for their children. Later, she started similar clubs in the Faroe Islands, Norway, Iran, India, and twice in the United States, where the Marstranders finally became citizens.

When Henning was sent to the coal mines in Birmingham, Alabama, Sigrid and Erna Xan met at last, and became "sisters" for life.

The Girl from Wisconsin

By Erna Oleson Xan

Just as Henning Marstrander asked Sigrid if she would follow him anywhere in the world, and she said, "Yes," so unbeknownst to them, John asked me the same question. But I, less adventuresome than Sigrid, replied, "John, dear, I will follow you anywhere, but don't you dare ask me to go to the Arctic or the desert!" Sigrid went to both with her man, and lived in such climates for years. I just had to follow mine around the good old U.S.A.

John was full of funny sayings. Once, in Chicago, during our engagement, strolling along on a date, he said, "Let's go window-shopping and get our wants dissatisfied."

On these occasions, we would pretend we were already married, and called each other "Professor" and "Mrs. Xan." Looking in the store windows, we furnished our future home, and dressed up for the elegant faculty receptions we knew would be our lot when we were really man and wife, and John was teaching in a college.

The first position, after the Master's degree, was at lovely old Sioux Falls College in South Dakota. At these social events one could always find the "Professor" standing up, talking with somebody. But he was aware of where I was. When I did appear through a door, he would reach out an arm, and without the slightest break in the conversation, draw my arm through his, and turning to his companion, say in the most courteous tone, "Have you met my lady?"

One time he couldn't find me anywhere and turned to a man he did not know very well, saying, "Have you seen my lady?"

The man, thinking he might be speaking of a titled woman, asked, "Oh, is your wife a Lady?"

John waited a moment, then replied, "Why, certainly! Isn't yours?"

John and I could never get over our meeting in Chicago. Born 6,000 miles away in Greece, he had come to America to attend Kalamazoo College, which was right across Lake Michigan from Waupaca (Wisconsin) high school where I went to school. Upon graduation, John went back to France to fight in World War I and was nearly killed. So, how was it that, one day in 1921, we met in that vast city? Whose lovely plan was this? On New Year's Day, 1921, coming into Chicago to begin a new job, how was it that I went to a telephone booth and engaged a room at a certain Eleanor Club for Girls, where three of John's older friends lived? At this time he was studying for a Master's degree in chemistry at the University of Chicago nearby.

These friends had heard John describe the girl he was looking for. Don't bring him a painted doll—she had to have naturally-rosy cheeks. (I blushed if someone looked at me.) She had to have naturally-curly blonde hair. (I rolled up my straight blonde hair every night of the world.) She had to be smart. (Well, I had been teaching country school!) On the third night in Chicago, the friends made a slick attempt to get us together. It didn't work. Three weeks later, he saw me alone and said to himself, "There's my wife!"

9

Erna Oleson Xan. Photograph by Darrell Henning.

Our courtship was fun, and we found things to celebrate all of our lives. But three were special.

One day, walking down 63rd Street we came upon a Greek import store. John's mouth flew open and he pointed to the window. I saw nothing but a small barrel of little withered "prunes." He rushed in and bought a carton of them. *Ugh!* They were ripe olives in *burning* brine! He had not had one since he left home, and he ate them like candy.

The next time we went window-shopping, we compromised on big black canned olives, which both of us relished. To the park! The can was opened and drained, and was placed between us on a newspaper. "Don't throw away the pits," John said. "Let's see who is the Piggie." So each put the pits on his or her side of the can. Of course, every now and then, John would call my attention to something passing by, and while I looked, he would slip a few pits over to my side. When the can was empty, of course, I would have the most, and lose the game. However, never underestimate a woman. I caught on to his tricks, and sneaked a few over to his side when he wasn't looking. All of our lives we played "Piggie" with a can of black olives, and celebrated our finding each other.

The second Celebration came after our marriage. It was introduced by Léonie Roussin, a French woman who lived next to us in a rooming house near the University, where John was now studying for his doctorate in chemistry. Léonie had run away from her home in Dinan, France, where her father had arranged a marriage to a man she hated. Now she was engaged to one of her language pupils, Morris Briggs, a big, jolly dealer in rare books. Léonie chattered away in French. We understood and haltingly replied, and we all became friends for life.

At one of her little card-table suppers, she put a spiny sort of green bulb on each plate, along with a dish of browned butter, a glass of milk, and a plate of plain brown bread. Puzzled, I looked down at the bulb. Nothing like that ever grew in Wisconsin! I watched the others pull leaf after leaf from the bulb, dip it in the butter, and draw it through their teeth to get the flesh at the end. Since I was slow and awkward at it, Léonie exclaimed: "N'aimez-vous pas les artichaux?" ("Do you not love artichokes?")

In the next moment I tasted what was to become for John and me another Celebration Food. Before I had finished cutting the "thistle" out of the bottom, and eaten the delicious, crunchy cup dipped in the brown butter, I was smitten for life. On that night, and all the rest of his life, when it came to eating that cup, John passed about a third of his onto my plate.

(N'aimez-vous pas les artichaux?)

John received his Ph.D. in Chemistry in June of 1926. Our first job after that was at Ottawa University, Ottawa, Kansas. By the next spring, John was raring to travel. I was taking swimming lessons. My sister, Henrietta, and her small daughter, Julia, were visiting us at the time. One day at lunch, John said, "Stay home with them today. Don't go to class."

"I can't miss class!" I cried. "Besides, little Julia will be taking a nap." And I hastened up to the gym.

On the way back, I heard a merry "Ooga, Ooga" toot behind me, and here came a brand new, shiny black Model T Ford, with John and Henrietta and Julia grinning through the windshield! John had bought a car, and *they* got the first ride.

"That will teach you to obey your husband," laughed John, as I climbed into the back seat. The moment school was out that spring, we were off to California.

Though he was now 34 years old, John had never driven a car, but the little Ford just rambled right along. Up the mountains, 'round the curves, over the burning sands. One time we lost a wheel. Another time the brakes gave out at the top of a canyon, and we descended 16 miles on "emergency" and "low gear."

But we didn't turn back. John had never forgotten the Golden State where he had trained for World War I. Now he was going to show me where we would spend our old age.

Besides, there were fields of artichokes, there were olive trees, and One Fine Day we came upon a fruit market with piled-up bins of big, fragrant, glossy, black cherries. Eight cents a quart! John jumped out and bought some. They were sweet, and juicy, and plump, and went Straight to The Spot. Sitting there in our very own first car, eating that quart of black cherries, both of us knew that we had found another Celebration Food.

John was a born teacher, and he loved young people. We never did have much money. We had just got started when the Depression hit. And John preferred teaching in small colleges, though at a lesser salary, so that he might have closer contact with his students.

So we could not indulge in our Celebration Foods every time they came on the market. They had to be "three for a dollar," or "reduced to 25 cents," or some other bargain. From then on, when he came home from the grocery, set the bag on the kitchen table, and kept the top closed with his hands, I knew that he had a special surprise.

11

"Guess!"

"Artichokes."

"Nope."

"Black Olives?"

"Nope."

"Black *Cherries!*"

At that he would open the bag, hand out a carton of big sweet-smelling fruit, kiss me and say, "For you, my Eno-Eno!" (A pet name he made up out of the letters of my name. His Eno-Eno, whom he had found 6,000 miles from home, and with whom he "celebrated joy.")

John's last position was at Howard College (now Samford University) in Birmingham, Alabama, where for 24 years he was Professor and Head of the Chemistry Department, taking the place of his dear old University of Chicago "buddy," Dr. John R. Sampey, Jr. We also inherited the love that the Sampeys left. The precious faculty members and the church were our "family." Our only daughter, Dixie Lee, was born in Birmingham.

John became famous for the number and accomplishments of his chemistry majors, and he received a national award. His students also initiated a college scholarship in his honor.

The Characters Eat

Nothing could be more fitting than for Erna Oleson Xan to write about foods and recipes. She's been doing it for quite some time. Born June 8, 1898, in Oshkosh, she attended Wisconsin schools and earned a master's degree in creative writing from the University of Michigan, where one of her professors commented: "Never have we had a student like you whose characters are always eating."

Mrs. Xan's three published books are *Wisconsin My Home*, from which excerpts are reprinted in this book; *Home for Good*, the story of her childhood on a Wisconsin farm; and *Time-Honored Norwegian Recipes*, co-authored with Sigrid Marstrander. Mrs. Xan wrote for the Birmingham News for eight years, and is an adviser and reviewer for The Christian Herald Family Bookshelf.

Norwegian thrift is expressed in this Norwegian tray cover: "Crumbs are also bread." Marion Nelson, director of Vesterheim, recalls from student days in Oslo that his hostess would ritualistically collect the crumbs from the table and place them in a box on the window sill saying "Fuglen og de fattige må også have sit." (Birds and the poor must also get their share.) Vesterheim collection.

Time-Honored Notes

By Erna Oleson Xan

Some things you may think are overdone. One is the almonds. These are imported, but when cookie- and cake-baking time comes, Norwegians must have their almonds.

Parsley is served on many vegetables. During the sunlit Norwegian summers, this green is grown in abundance. In winter, some raise it in a pot in the deep window-sill. Home-grown root vegetables are kept in the cellar. Almost everything fresh, like lettuce and tomatoes, is imported from warmer climates. The use of parsley must have contributed much to the health in the long dark winter months.

Eggs were scarce in Norway, and high in price. Once when Sigrid was a girl, a neighbor asked her to take care of her little boy for the afternoon. The pay was an egg, and Sigrid triumphantly carried it home. Eggs were usually eaten only on Sunday morning, otherwise saved for baking.

Chickens are still expensive in Norway. But there are plenty of fish, lambs, pigs, and cows. The old recipes were heavy with butter and cream. Nowadays the people often substitute their excellent margarine, except in *Berlinerkranser* cookies at Christmas.

Rye, oats and barley were the most common grains of the country. Most wheat had to be imported, as was corn, an animal food.

The cookbooks that Sigrid carried around the world are now brown and loose in the binding. All are around eighty-five years old but they hold the favorite Norwegian recipes still used in Norway. Sigrid has made twenty trips home, and she knows.

She cooked by the gram and kilo scales. Our hardest problem in writing this little cookbook was to translate from the metric system to the English cups and spoonfuls. The credit for these recipes goes entirely to Sigrid. My task was to make them fit the American system.

For instance, recipes called for all kinds of odd measures: *barneskje* (child's spoon); *teskje* (half a teaspoon); *spiseskje* (one soup spoon); *en smule* (a crumb of this or that); *knap en liter* (not quite a liter).

All the English measurements in our book are level and standard.

The old books seldom mentioned salt in a recipe. I suppose they thought anybody knew enough to add it. They often required that one beat the eggs and sugar or butter for an hour. We settled for "till light and lemon-colored."

No exact oven temperatures were given. "Hot" and "medium warm" we had to translate according to Sigrid's experience, for she has made over and over again almost all the dishes in this book.

Two reference works we could not have done without were Dr. Einer Haugen's excellent *Norwegian-English Dictionary* and Irma Rombauer's *Joy of Cooking*, which has been my treasured cooking guide for a generation.

My mother, Thurine Oleson, used to say "Bidden Food is as Good as Eaten." It means, "The honor is in the asking." So we bid you to come and eat, and do not forget our dear old Norwegian table prayer beginning *"I Jesus' Navn."*

'I Jesus' Navn'

I Jesus' Navn går vi til bords,
Spiser, drikker på dit ord,
Dig til aere, os til gavn,
Så får vi mat i Jesus' Navn.

In Jesus' Name we take our place
To eat and drink upon Thy grace.
To Thy honor and our gain
We take our food in Jesus' Name.

"Giv os Idag vort daglige Brød" *(Give us this day our daily bread).* Vesterheim collection.

Soups and Porridges

Trondheim Fruit Soup
Trondhjemsuppe

2   quarts water
½   cup uncooked rice
1   cup seedless raisins
1   teaspoon flour
¾   cup half-and-half cream
     juice of ½ lemon
½   cup raspberry or strawberry juice
     (canned or fresh)

Use a thick-bottomed kettle. Bring water to a boil; add rice, stirring occasionally. Cook for ½ hour, add raisins, and cook another 15 minutes.

Make a paste of the flour and a little cream. Add the rest of the cream and lemon juice and stir. Add to the soup and let it boil up. Take off the heat and add the fruit juice. Serve hot. Serves 6.

A delicious luncheon or supper dish served with bread and butter or as a dinner dessert.

Rhubarb Soup
Rabarbrasuppe
Cold soup for summertime supper.

4   cups young rhubarb
1   cup water, divided
6   tablespoons sugar
¼   teaspoon cinnamon
1   teaspoon cornstarch

Wash rhubarb and cut into ½-inch lengths. Place in saucepan with ½ cup water, sugar and cinnamon. Cook, covered, until tender, about 15 minutes. Mix cornstarch with the remaining ½ cup water. Remove boiling rhubarb from stove, add cornstarch and water mixture, stir. Put back on heat for another boil, then take off the stove and chill the soup. Serves 4.

Serve cold with zwieback broken into it, and more sugar if desired. This soup has the distinction of being served after the main supper dish instead of before it.

Apple Soup
Eplesuppe

1½ pounds tart apples
2 quarts cold water
¼ teaspoon cinnamon
1 slice lemon
½ cup sugar or more to taste
1 tablespoon cornstarch dissolved in
    ¼ cup water

Peel apples thinly; core and slice. Put in the cold water immediately so they will not darken. Add cinnamon and lemon and cook gently. When they are tender, stir in sugar, then add cornstarch dissolved in water, and bring quickly to a boil again. Serve cold. Serves 6.

This soup also is eaten after *the main meal. Many like to drop broken pieces of zwieback in it.*

Split Pea Soup
Ertesuppe
For Henning's Saturday night.

1 cup split peas
1 small ham hock
2 quarts water
2 medium-sized carrots
½ small onion
   salt to taste

Wash peas and soak overnight in enough water to cover. In the morning, boil the ham hock in 2 quarts of water for ½ hour. Add the peas and soaking water to the ham hock kettle, cover and boil slowly until the peas are mushy, about 1 hour.

Lift out the ham hock. Scrape and slice carrots, chop onion fine, and add both to the cooked peas. Salt if necessary. Cook for another 30 minutes. If there is meat on the ham hock, chop fine and return it to the soup. Serves 6.

Be sure to have Everyday Pancakes

(Almindelige Pannekaker) *to serve with this on Saturday night, and save the last one for the dog. One of Sigrid's cousins in Norway had a St. Bernard dog. He would sit by the table patiently all through the meal and wait for his. When the meal was over, they lifted the cake above his head, he opened his big mouth, the cake went in, he closed his lips and there was no other movement. It just slid down.*

Cauliflower Soup
Blomkålsuppe

3 tablespoons butter
2 medium carrots, sliced fine
¼ cup coarsely cut parsley
3 tablespoons flour
1½ quarts cauliflower stock, heated
    (left from other *blomkål* recipes)
½ cup half-and-half cream
   salt to taste

In a 2-quart saucepan, melt butter and add carrots and parsley. Cook slowly for 5 minutes, stirring frequently. Sprinkle flour over vegetables and stir well. Add 2 cups heated stock and stir until it makes a smooth sauce. Add the rest of stock and boil until carrots are well done. If there should be any cauliflower left from previous meals, cut the stems in fine pieces and add them along with any leftover "flowers." Stir in the cream and salt and serve. Serves 6.

This is not only delicious but it costs almost nothing.

Butter Porridge

Smørgrøt

For delicate stomachs.

¾ cup butter
2 cups flour
2 quarts milk
1 teaspoon salt
6 teaspoons butter, approximately
  sugar and cinnamon mixture

Melt butter in a large saucepan. Sift in the flour to make a smooth paste. Boil the milk in another pan and then stir gradually into the butter mixture to make it smooth. Boil 5 minutes. Add salt, and supper is ready. Place in individual bowls, make a "butter eye" (a large dab of butter) in the top and sprinkle with sugar and cinnamon mixture. Serve with a glass of milk. Serves 6.

Rice Porridge

Risengrynsgrøt

Christmas and New Year's fare.

2 quarts milk
¾ cup uncooked rice
½ teaspoon salt
1½ tablespoons butter, divided
   sugar and cinnamon mixture

If you do not have a big double boiler, make one by placing the pan into a larger pan of water, for this porridge takes two hours to cook. Boil the milk. As it boils, stir in the rice, salt and 1 tablespoon butter. Cover and stir occasionally so that it does not stick to the bottom. When done, pile into a serving bowl, put a "butter eye" in the middle and pass it around along with the sugar and cinnamon. Serve with a glass of milk or berry juice. Serves 6.

This grøt has been a tradition for Christmas Eve and New Year's Eve for generations, but it can be served any time during the year. During the holidays, one almond is buried in the grøt and the one who gets it is supposed to be the happiest person during the coming year. Leftovers can be utilized in many ways, especially to make Rice Cream (see Desserts).

Cream Porridge

Rømmegrøt

Norway's famous Midsummer Day's treat.

3 cups whipping cream
2 cups flour, divided
8 cups milk, boiling hot
½ teaspoon salt
  sugar and cinnamon mixture

In a heavy saucepan, heat the cream for 10 minutes, stirring frequently so that it will not burn. Sift in ½ cup flour, beating to make a thin porridge. Let it boil slowly until the butterfat starts to rise. Reduce heat and skim all butter off with a spoon. Put it in a cup to keep warm. Now, gradually sift in the rest of the flour, turning up the heat a little and stirring very well. Add hot milk gradually, stirring all the while. Add salt. *Rømmegrøt* thickens as it stands.

Pile it into a large serving bowl, make a dent in the top and pour some of the butterfat into it. It will run down the sides of the porridge like lava on Vesuvius. Pass the *Rømmegrøt* bowl and the butter cup and let each one help himself. Sprinkle on the cinnamon and sugar mixture, and eat! A glass of milk or berry juice is good with this. Serves 6.

Sigrid contends that you can make Rømmegrøt from commercial cream, but it does not taste the same as when the cream comes straight from the cow.

Norwegian utensils for fisk og kjøtt (fish and meat) at Vesterheim, the Norwegian-American Museum, Decorah, Iowa. Boiling has been the traditional way of preparing fresh fish and meat in Norway. The limited number of spices used here were ground in a mortar and pestle of wood, glass, iron or brass. Much of the meat and fish was chopped and ground for serving as fishballs, meatballs, puddings or sausages. This was done in wood bowls with various kinds of choppers and stompers. The work was continued until a fine paste had been obtained. Coarse grinding, as is common in America, was seldom done in Norway. Sausages were filled with the aid of a small funnel made from wood or horn. Puddings were sometimes pressed into fancy molds such as the fish mold for fish pudding. Pewter and ceramic platters were luxury items since most of them were imported. Serving was from kettles or wood slabs.

Photograph by Joan Liffring-Zug

Fish and Meat

Fish and Shrimp in Pastry Shells

Fiskeboller i Mørdeig

Pastry shells:
- 3 cups flour
- 1 teaspoon baking powder
- ½ teaspoon salt
- 1¼ cups butter
- ½ cup ice water

Sift flour, baking powder and salt together into a mixing bowl. Cut the butter into it with a pastry blender. Sprinkle over it the ice water and blend. Chill the dough. To roll it out, use a stockinet-covered rolling pin with a canvas-covered board or plastic pastry sheet. Flour both lightly. Roll dough as thin as you can handle it.

To shape the shells, lay a saucer on the dough and cut a circle a little bit bigger. Fit this circle on the outside of a 6-ounce ovenproof glass custard cup. Prick top with a fork. Place upside down on a cookie sheet. Bake at 450° F. about 10 minutes. Take out when light brown. Cool and carefully remove from cup.

Filling:

Surprise! No longer do you have to buy fish fresh from the ocean and work all day preparing it. Go to your delicatessen and buy:
- 1 can Norwegian fish balls
- 2 cans small shrimp

White Sauce:
- 3 tablespoons butter
- 2 tablespoons flour
- 1 cup fish stock (add milk if there isn't a cupful)
- ¼ cup half-and-half cream
- ½ teaspoon salt
- parsley for garnish

Drain fish balls and save the juice. Cut the balls into ½-inch pieces. Drain shrimp.

In a saucepan, melt the butter and blend in flour till smooth. Gradually add the cup of fish stock, stirring until satin smooth. Add cream and salt, cubed fish balls and ⅔ of shrimp. Cook slowly, stirring occasionally, until heated through. When ready to serve, pile the fish-shrimp mixture into pastry shells and decorate the top with remaining shrimp.

Sigrid says, "Do not forget to put a sprig of parsley right in the middle of the top!"

Ladies rave over this luncheon dish. In Norway they served flatbrød *or buttered toast, tomato wedges and celery pieces with it. Coffee, of course. If you serve* Rødgrøt med Fløte *for dessert, you have a truly Norwegian luncheon.*

Violence in the Kitchen

She breaks an egg
She beats it up
She whips the cream
She cracks the nuts
She chops the cabbage
She pounds the steak
She punches the dough
She cuts the bread
She scalds the milk
She mashes the potatoes
She shakes the lettuce
She squeezes the lemon
And *slaps* the supper on the table

Erna Oleson Xan

18

Poached Fish

Kokt Fisk

Cooked the last minute before serving.

3 pounds frozen fillet of cod or
     haddock (defrosted)
   tomato wedges for garnish
   melted butter and chopped parsley
     or Hollandaise Sauce

Cut each fillet into individual servings. Drop fillets into a kettle of boiling salted water. Bring again to a boil, reduce heat and simmer for 10 to 12 minutes. (Boiling ruins the fine flavor.) When done, lift fillets out with a slotted spoon. Save the stock to make Hollandaise Sauce, if desired. Serve the fish on a warm platter. Decorate with tomato wedges. Serves 6.

In Norway, the traditional way is to serve poached fish with melted butter into which chopped parsley has been stirred, or Hollandaise Sauce can be served.

Hollandaise Sauce

Hollandsk Saus

Will not curdle.

1 tablespoon flour
¼ teaspoon salt
¾ cup water
6 tablespoons butter
4 egg yolks
½ cup fish stock
2 tablespoons lemon juice

Mix flour and salt. Put water in saucepan, add flour mixture and bring to boil. Take off the heat and cool. Partly melt the butter and beat into the flour mixture, then beat in egg yolks, one at a time. Stir in the fish stock. Put the pan back on the heat and keep on beating until sauce thickens. Take off heat immediately and stir in the lemon juice.

Serve over Poached Fish with pars-
leyed boiled potatoes and glazed carrots.

Although this sauce comes from Holland, it has acquired through the years a Norwegian name. Recipes have a wonderful way of "jumping the border" without passport but are always welcomed by any country.

When you cook fish, you might want to cook an extra pound at the same time so that you will have enough for a later Fiskegratin, or Fish Soufflé. In the meantime, keep fish covered in cold stock in the refrigerator.

Fish Soufflé

Fiskegratin

5 tablespoons butter
3 tablespoons flour
2 cups milk
½ cup half-and-half cream
½ pound cold poached cod or haddock (can be leftovers)
4 eggs
¼ teaspoon salt
¼ teaspoon grated nutmeg
½ cup crushed zwieback or dry bread crumbs.

Melt the butter in a saucepan. Blend in the flour until it makes a smooth paste. Slowly add the milk and cream and stir until smooth. Finely chop the fish and stir into saucepan. Beat eggs until light and foamy and fold into the fish mixture. Sprinkle in the salt and nutmeg and blend.

Grease an ovenproof dish. Spoon the soufflé into it and sprinkle the zwieback or crumbs on top. Bake at 375°F. for 45 minutes to 1 hour, or until nicely browned on top.

Norwegians usually serve this with melted butter, but Asparagus Sauce adds a very special taste.

Asparagus Sauce
Aspargessaus

1 tablespoon butter
1 tablespoon flour
2 cups fish stock
3 tablespoon half-and-half cream
½ cup canned asparagus tops and
    stems, drained and chopped

Melt the butter in a saucepan; blend in the flour until smooth. Little by little add the fish stock until all is satin smooth, then stir in the cream. Fold in the asparagus.

This is a good recipe because canned chopped pieces of asparagus, which you can get any season and are inexpensive, are just the thing for it.

Fish Balls and Fish Pudding
Fiskeboller, Fiskepudding

Once a month for years, we (Sigrid and Erna) got together at one of our homes for a Fish Ball dinner. It was our "Sisterhood Ceremony" in honor of our pure-blooded Norwegian heritage and our friendship. While we ate, we told each other stories of our ancestors and our people and things that happened when we visited the beautiful land.
—S.G.M.

fresh fish (haddock is best)
1 heaping teaspoon potato flour
   salt to taste
2 cups milk
2 cups cream
   nutmeg to taste

Work in a cool place to avoid spoilage of the fresh fish. Clean the fish and rinse well. Scrape meat from bones and pat dry in a cloth. Reserve skin and bones to make fish stock. Then mash fish fine on a board. The scraped fish can also be put through a grinder 5 times.

To a deep soup-plate amount of fish, add the above amounts of potato flour and salt, and stir well for ½ hour. Add milk and cream a spoonful at a time until desired consistency is reached; if you are going to make pudding, the mixture can be a little softer than for fish balls. Season with a little nutmeg.

For Fish Balls, make a stock by boiling the reserved skin and bones in salted water for 10 minutes. Strain. Before boiling all the balls, try one first to see if it holds together. Drop teaspoonfuls of the fish mixture into the boiling stock. They will rise to the top when done, about 7 or 8 minutes. They will keep up to several weeks if covered in stock in a cold place.

For Fish Pudding, put the fish mixture into a greased and floured baking dish. Place this in a pan of boiling water in a 350°F. oven for 45 minutes.

Fish Pudding and Fish Balls can be covered by a white sauce with capers, shrimp, celery or lobster. Serve with mealy boiled potatoes, cooked carrots and peas, and, of course, lots of chopped parsley sprinkled over it.

This breakfast doily in satin stitch has the simple message "Spis godt stegt brød" translated is "Eat well toasted bread." Vesterheim collection.

Herring Salad
Sildesalat

3 salted herring
 chopped cooked beef or veal to
  equal the amount of herring
2 large potatoes, cooked and cubed
2 medium carrots, grated
1 small onion, finely chopped
¼ cup chopped sweet pickle
1 cup cream
1 teaspoon vinegar
1 tablespoon sugar
 salt and pepper to taste

For decoration:
2 eggs hard-cooked, whites and
  yolks chopped separately
1 cup canned beets, dried on paper
  towel and chopped fine
½ cup grated carrots
½ cup sliced stuffed green olives
 sprig of parsley

Soak the herring overnight. In the morning, throw soaking water away and cover with fresh water. Boil 10 minutes, drain and cool. Chop herring into small pieces and place in a mixing bowl. Add the chopped beef, potatoes, carrots, onion and pickle. In another bowl mix cream, vinegar, sugar, salt and pepper. Stir well into the herring mixture.

Run cold water into *deep* bowl, leave it until bowl is chilled, and pour it out. Pack the salad into bowl, chill for several hours, then turn out onto a platter.

Decorate salad in "watermelon stripes," alternating colors—egg whites, beets, egg yolks, then carrots, and repeating this order until done. To make divisions between the stripes, place a ½-inch-wide strip of paper between them while you are working and remove it as you go. Decorate the top with sliced olives and parsley. Serves 8 to 10.

Makes a beautiful main dish for a buffet supper.

Boneless Birds
Benløse Fugle

3 pounds flank steak (as thick as the
  little finger)
1 teaspoon salt
½ teaspoon pepper
¼ teaspoon ground cloves
 1-by 1-inch strips salt pork (Raw
  marrow is better. Finely chopped
  suet will do.)
 flour
2 tablespoons butter

Pound the flank steak with a meat hammer until it is an even thickness all the way across. Cut into 3- by 4-inch pieces. Mix salt, pepper and cloves. On each piece of meat lay a strip of salt pork or 2 teaspoons of marrow or suet. Sprinkle with the salt, pepper and clove mixture. Roll up the meat and tie with cord or heavy white thread. Roll "birds" in flour and brown in the butter.

Sauce:
2 tablespoons butter
1½ tablespoons flour
3 cups broth
4 tablespoons sour cream

Make the sauce in another pan. Brown the butter slowly, blend in the flour, and add the broth very slowly to make a smooth sauce. Bring it to a boil and place the "birds" in it. Cover tightly and simmer for 1 hour. Add sour cream and simmer a few minutes more. What cooks down will make the gravy. If necessary, thin with a little water. Serves 6.

Meat and Soup

Kjøttsuppe

Hearty two-course meal for a cold day.

4½ quarts water
1 large beef soup bone, split in two
1 teaspoon salt
2 pounds beef stew meat
4 carrots, scrubbed and trimmed
2 parsnips, scrubbed and trimmed
2 green onions with tops, cut up
2 stalks celery, with leaves, cut up
½ cup chopped parsley
5 or 6 boiled potatoes

Place the water, beef bone and salt in a large kettle and simmer for 2 hours. Skim off scum as it rises. As water boils away, add more.

Remove the beef bone and put in the stew meat. Cook for 1 hour, then add the whole carrots and parsnips and the cut-up onions and celery. Boil slowly for another hour. At the end, there should be 2 quarts of liquid.

This will now make 2 courses. Lift out the meat and put it into a dish to keep warm. Reserve it for the second course.

The first course is soup. Cut up the cooked parsnips and carrots and return them to the soup. Serve with parsley sprinkled on top. The following dumplings make a delicious addition to the soup if you wish to include them.

Dumplings:

Brødboller

1 tablespoon butter
1 egg
1 cup milk
1 cup crushed zwieback
2 teaspoons sugar
¼ teaspoon ground cardamom
   dash of ground cinnamon

Beat the butter until soft, beat and add the egg. Add milk and stir. Mix together the zwieback, sugar, cardamom and cinnamon. Stir gradually into milk mixture. Be sure the dough is stiff enough to make a ball with a spoon. If not, add a little more crushed zwieback. Dip the teaspoon into water, then into the dough. Immerse spoonful of dough in the boiling soup and the ball will come off. As soon as it rises to the top, the dumpling is done.

Serve reserved meat with Onion Sauce and boiled potatoes as a second course.

Onion Sauce:

Løksaus

4 tablespoons butter, divided
2 tablespoons flour
1 cup hot milk
¼ teaspoon salt
   dash of pepper
1 medium-sized onion
½ cup meat-soup stock
2 tablespoons cream
¼ teaspoon sugar

Make a white sauce: Over low heat, melt 2 tablespoons butter and blend in the flour to make a paste. Add milk gradually, stirring the while, then add salt and pepper.

Chop onion very fine. Put 2 tablespoons butter in a saucepan and add the onion. Cook slowly until onions are transparent but not brown. Slowly blend in the stock and white sauce. Simmer for 15 minutes. Strain sauce through a colander. Reheat, and add cream and sugar. Pour this sauce over the meat. Serves 6 generously.

Pork Tenderloin

Svinekam

An elegant company dinner.

pork loin, one rib for each person
1 teaspoon salt
½ teaspoon pepper
2 cups water
potatoes and other vegetables
Gravy:
2 tablespoons meat drippings
2 tablespoons flour
1 cup vegetable stock or hot water
Garnishes:
tomato wedges
lettuce leaves
parsley sprigs

Have the butcher cut the loin just through the bone at each rib for easier cutting and serving. Sprinkle with salt and pepper and place dry in a shallow pan. Bake at 350°F. 30 to 35 minutes per pound. When loin begins to brown, add 2 cups water. When the meat begins to recede from the bone, it is well done. (Never serve pink pork.)

Remove the meat to a large platter. Finish cutting through to make individual servings but keep it together like a whole loin. Place in a warming oven.

To make gravy: In the roasting pan, drain off the fat except 2 tablespoons. Heat this; stir in the flour until smooth. Slowly add the stock or hot water and stir until gravy is satiny.

While the meat is baking, prepare a variety of vegetables to your taste. Parsleyed potatoes, of course, will be served in a separate dish. Carrots may be cooked, or Brussels sprouts, long green beans, asparagus, cauliflower or peas. Just before serving, arrange vegetables artistically around the pork loin, decorating alternately with wedges of tomato, a few crisp lettuce leaves and sprigs of parsley. Serve gravy in a separate dish.

When this platter is borne to the table, it reminds the visitor to Norway of the Medieval dishes that were "set before the King!"

Mutton and Cabbage

Får i Kål

1 medium head cabbage
6 pounds mutton breast or leg, or lamb
1½ tablespoons salt
1 teaspoon black pepper
½ cup flour
1½ quarts boiling water

To prepare the cabbage, cut in quarters and remove core. Cut each quarter crosswise in 6 pieces. Plunge into salted boiling water, then place in cold water. Drain.

This is a layered dish. Choose a large heavy kettle. Cut the raw meat into serving pieces, using the fattest for the bottom layer. Place a third of the meat in kettle. Mix the salt, pepper and flour. Sprinkle a third of this mixture on the meat. Then lay on a third of the cabbage. Repeat the layers (meat, flour, cabbage) until you have used it all.

Pour 1½ quarts boiling water into the kettle. Cover with a tight lid and bring it to a boil. Then reduce heat and simmer for 2½ hours. (Stir a couple of times so that the top layer goes to the bottom.) Add more salt or pepper if necessary. If too much fat rises, skim it off.

This is a big dish, and it makes tasty leftovers. In Norway it is said that the seventh day is the best. Norwegians use 1½ tablespoons whole black peppercorns, which make a pretty appearance in the dish, but which have to be fished out as you eat it.

I said to Sigrid, "What do you serve with this dish?" She looked me straight in the eye and said, "Boiled parsleyed potatoes!"

Norsk Folkemuseum, Oslo, Norway. Photograph by Darrell Henning.

Meat Cakes
Kjøttkaker

3 pounds stew meat
¼ pound fresh pork
1 cup milk, boiled and cooled
2 tablespoons cornstarch
1 teaspoon salt
  dash of ground ginger
  dash of nutmeg
¼ teaspoon pepper
  flour for coating cakes
6 tablespoons butter, divided
2 tablespoons flour
2 cups broth
  salt to taste

Have butcher grind the meat and pork together three times.

Bring milk to boil and cool it. Mix cornstarch with salt and spices and work thoroughly into the meat. Then little by little add the cold boiled milk. Shape the meat into 2½-inch cakes about ½ inch thick. Coat them on both sides in a little flour. Melt 2 tablespoons butter in a skillet and brown the cakes, turning carefully. Remove to a bowl.

Melt the remaining 4 tablespoons of butter in the skillet, blend in 2 tablespoons flour and stir until smooth and brown. Little by little add the broth. Cook, stirring constantly, until smooth and satiny. Add salt to taste. Add the meat cakes and cook for 8 to 10 minutes. Serves 6.

24

Vegetables

Mealy Boiled Potatoes
Kokt Poteter
No dinner is complete without this!

1   potato for each person
½   teaspoon salt
    parsley, chopped

Peel potatoes very thinly and place in boiling salted water. When they are done, pour water off. (Save it for soup or gravy, or just drink it. Do not throw it away.) Put the pan back on the stove over low heat and shake the pan to dry the potatoes, making them very mealy. Turn off the heat, leave potatoes in the pan, covered with a folded towel across the top. Put the lid back on and keep warm until serving time. The towel will absorb all the rest of the moisture. At mealtime, sprinkle with chopped parsley.

Mealy boiled potatoes go with any meat or fish dish. (If you boil potatoes in their jackets, of course you will throw the water away.)

Greta's Chestnut Potatoes
Gretas Kastanjepoteter

3   small new potatoes for each person
    butter

Wash and brush potatoes well. Put them in a greased shallow pan. Bake at 400°F. until they are crisp on the outside and well done inside. Serve warm in a napkin in a dish. (Don't ask us why the napkin.) Serve with butter. They look like chestnuts and taste delicious.

Greta's Potatoes
Gretas Poteter

8   raw potatoes
    salt to taste

Peel, wash and dry potatoes. Place them in a greased shallow pan and bake at 400°F. until they are brown and crisp on the outside and done on the inside. When serving, sprinkle with salt. Serve with cold meat and cheese.

Potato Rolls
Potetesruletter

6   to 8 boiled potatoes, cooled
3   tablespoons melted butter
1   egg yolk
½   teaspoon salt
    dash of pepper
2   teaspoons cornstarch
1   egg white
    zwieback or bread crumbs
    deep fat for frying

Put potatoes through a sieve. Add melted butter and egg yolk, salt and pepper. Sprinkle with cornstarch and mix well. Roll out in finger shapes, dip in slightly beaten egg white, and then in the crumbs. Place them singly on a large pan to rest for 15 minutes. Then fry in deep fat until light brown. Take up with slotted spoon and let them drain on paper towel. Serve hot. Serves 6.

Makes a fine little side dish for cold meat, tomatoes and lettuce. Flatbrød is good with this meal.

Boiled Cauliflower
Kokt Blomkål

1 head cauliflower
2 quarts water
½ teaspoon salt
3 tablespoons butter, melted
  parsley, finely chopped

Take off the cauliflower's big outer leaves. Cut the stalk off to about 1 inch and cut a deep cross on the end to make it cook quicker. Place the cauliflower in some cold salted water for a while to drive out any insects.

Boil 2 quarts of water with ½ teaspoon salt; put the cauliflower in, head up, and boil for 3 minutes. Take it out of the water; pour cold water over it to cool it. This keeps the cauliflower white. Place it back into the boiling water, head down this time, and boil for 20 minutes. (Be careful not to cook it to pieces!) Drain and save the water for Cauliflower Soup. Serve head of cauliflower on a platter with melted butter poured over, and sprinkle with parsley. Serves 6.

Cauliflower Soufflé
Blomkålgratin

1 medium-sized cauliflower
½ cup butter
1 cup flour
1⅔ cups hot milk
4 egg yolks
4 egg whites, stiffly beaten
  salt to taste
⅛ teaspoon nutmeg

Boil cauliflower according to previous recipe, but remove from water when not quite done.

In another pan, melt butter, add flour and stir until smooth. Then add hot milk slowly and stir until smooth. Cool. Add egg yolks one at a time. Add salt to taste

and the nutmeg. Fold in stiffly beaten egg whites. Separate cauliflower into flowerets (not too small) and fold them carefully into the batter. Spoon into buttered baking dish (oven-to-table ware), and bake at 325° F. for about 30 minutes.

Make a white sauce according to the one used with the Cauliflower and Shrimp recipe, and pass it during the serving. Serves 6.

This is a good luncheon dish.

Cauliflower with Shrimp
Blomkål med Reker

1 head cauliflower
1 teaspoon salt
1 pound cleaned fresh, frozen or
  canned shrimp
White Sauce:
2 tablespoons butter
2 tablespoons flour
1 cup hot milk
¼ teaspoon salt

Cook cauliflower according to Boiled Cauliflower recipe. Save water for Cauliflower Soup.

If using raw shrimp, cook according to directions on package. If canned shrimp, drain off liquid.

Make a white sauce in a double boiler: melt butter, stir in flour, hot milk and salt. Cook until thickened, stirring frequently. When done, stir in shrimp and heat. Place cauliflower on a platter, and just before serving, pour over it the shrimp-in-sauce. Serves 6.

Served with buttered toast, lettuce, tomato and hot coffee, this is a big favorite luncheon dish for ladies.

Red Cabbage
Surkål

1 large head red cabbage
2 tablespoons butter, divided
1¼ teaspoons caraway seeds
1 tablespoon flour
1 teaspoon salt
2 cups meat stock or water
1 tablespoon vinegar
1 tablespoon sugar

Cut away the core of the cabbage. Soak the head in cold salted water for 10 minutes and drain. Shred into fine strips. Grease bottom of kettle with 1 tablespoon butter. Then layer alternately the cabbage, caraway seeds and little dots of butter. Sprinkle in the flour and salt for each layer. Add stock or water. You should barely see it below the cabbage. Cover and boil for 1½ hours, stirring frequently. Do not let it boil dry.

Before serving, add vinegar and sugar and stir well. If necessary, add more salt to taste. Serves 6.

Good with any kind of pork dish or other meats. Surkål *makes a hit wherever it goes. The dish goes around and around the table until it is empty, and nobody cares if she gets to be the "old maid."*

Glazed Carrots
Glaserte Gulerøtter

6 medium-sized carrots
2 cups boiling water
1 teaspoon salt
4 tablespoons butter
2 teaspoons sugar
1 tablespoon finely chopped parsley

Scrape and trim carrots and cut each into four pieces. Place in a saucepan and pour boiling water over them; add salt, butter and sugar. Cover with a lid, and let boil until the carrots are almost done and water is almost evaporated. Shake the pan so that the carrots are turned and glazed all over. Sprinkle with chopped parsley. Serves 6.

"Parsley? Again?" I asked Sigrid. "Don't you think we ought to omit it if we are having it on something else?"

Sigrid replied, "I can't see why! Both carrots and parsley are good for the eyes."

Carrots with Lemon
Gulerøtter med Citron

1 pound carrots
2 tablespoons butter
2 teaspoons chopped parsley
  juice of half a lemon
  salt and pepper to taste

Wash and scrape carrots. Cut in slices. Boil in salted water to cover till tender. Drain and put back over heat to dry, shaking them the while. Add butter, parsley, lemon juice, a little salt and pepper, and stir it all together. Serves 6.

A mother cooking porridge finds that she is getting an extra draft on the fire from a nisse *(elf). The inscription* "Hjelp i huset" *means "Help in the house."* Vesterheim collection.

Parsnip Balls
Pastinakboller

7 medium-sized parsnips
1 egg, separated
   salt and pepper to taste
2 tablespoons flour
1 cup dry bread crumbs
2 tablespoons butter for pan frying
   or deep fat for frying

Scrub parsnips and scrape well. Remove stems and tails. Boil in salted water to cover until tender. Drain and dry them over heat, shaking constantly. Mash well. Add beaten egg yolk, salt and pepper, and stir in flour. Cool. Fold in the beaten egg white. Shape into 1½-inch balls. Roll in bread crumbs and either brown in butter in the skillet or fry in deep fat until golden brown. Serves 6.

Mashed Rutabaga
Kålrabistappe

4 four-inch strips salt pork
1 big rutabaga
3 or 4 medium potatoes
¼ cup margarine
½ cup hot milk
   pepper to taste

Boil the salt pork for ½ hour and remove from the water. Peel vegetables and cut in small pieces. Place rutabaga in the pork water and cook for 1 hour, then add the potatoes and cook for 20 minutes more. Drain off water. Mash vegetables very well; add margarine, hot milk and pepper. Beat until light and fluffy. Keep warm in a covered kettle while you fry the salt pork.

When serving, place the heap of mashed rutabaga on a platter, surrounded by the fried pork. Rutabaga can take the place of potato with roast pork, pork sausage or corned beef. Serves 4.

Onion Soufflé
Løk Souffle

3 medium onions
2 tablespoons butter
1 tablespoon flour
½ cup milk
¼ teaspoon salt
   dash of paprika
3 egg yolks, slightly beaten
3 egg whites, stiffly beaten

Boil onions until tender and then press through a colander. In a saucepan, melt butter. Stir in the flour to make a paste, and add the milk gradually. Then add the onion pulp, salt and paprika. Bring to a boil and add egg yolks. Lastly, fold in the stiffly beaten egg whites.

Grease a baking dish with butter. Pour in the soufflé and put the dish in another shallow pan of hot water. Bake at 350° F. for 25 to 30 minutes. Serve immediately. Serves 4.

Sugar Peas in Pods
Sukkererter

1 quart young peas in pods
1 tablespoon butter
2 teaspoons flour
2 teaspoons finely chopped parsley
½ teaspoon sugar
¼ teaspoon salt

Wash pods and remove stems and strings. Cut diagonally in 1-inch lengths. Cover with salted water and boil until tender. When done, drain, and save a cup of the liquid. In saucepan, melt butter and stir in the flour to make a paste. Add the pot liquid slowly and bring to a boil. Add the chopped parsley, sugar and salt, and stir into the peas. Serves 6.

Norwegian utensils for lefse og flat-brød at Vesterheim, the Norwegian-American Museum, Decorah, Iowa. The birch root basket was used for storing large rounds of flatbread. The utensils include flour and salt boxes, scoops for flour, a dough bowl, rolling pins for lefse and flatbread, a potato masher and grinder for making lefse, container for flatbread, and rollers. The wrought iron lefse grill was used in the fireplace.

Photograph by Joan Liffring-Zug.

Breads and Pancakes

Christmas Bread
Julekake

1 cup butter
¾ cup sugar (reserve 2 teaspoons for later use)
2 eggs
2 egg yolks
1 teaspoon salt
½ teaspoon ground cardamom
1 cup whole milk
2 packages dry yeast
4 cups sifted flour
1 cup seedless raisins
1 cup finely chopped citron
2 egg whites, beaten slightly

In a bowl, cream butter and sugar until light and lemon-colored. Beat the eggs and egg yolks, add to butter mixture and stir well. Add salt and cardamom.

Heat milk to lukewarm. Pour into a big bowl and sprinkle yeast on it. Add the reserved 2 teaspoons of sugar and stir. When the yeast has bubbled up, add alternately the flour and the butter mixture, beating with a wooden spoon until smooth. Cover and let stand in a warm place until double in bulk. Turn onto a floured board and knead until smooth and elastic. Lastly, knead in the raisins and citron.

If this is going to be just one big cake, place the dough into a greased 9-inch tube pan; if two, put into greased loaf pans. Let the dough rise again, covered with wax paper and a cloth, until double in bulk. Preheat oven to 350° F. Just before placing in oven brush the dough carefully with the egg whites to make a glaze. Bake for 50 to 60 minutes.

It is traditional in Norway to serve this for Christmas breakfast or afternoon coffee.

Rye Bread
Rugbrød
The daily bread of Norway.

1 cup milk
1 package dry yeast
1 teaspoon sugar
4 cups rye flour
½ teaspoon salt
2 teaspoons caraway seeds, optional
½ cup lukewarm water

Bring milk to boiling and cool to lukewarm. Pour ¼ cup into a bowl, sprinkle the yeast and sugar on it, and stir in 2 tablespoons of the flour. Let it bubble and rise for 15 minutes in a warm place.

In another bowl, sift the flour and salt. Add caraway seeds. Add the lukewarm water and milk and work to a fine dough. Add the yeast mixture and knead on a floured board for 15 minutes. Place dough in a greased bowl and turn dough upside down. Cover with waxed paper and a towel and let rise in a warm place for ¾ to 1 hour.

Knead it again with a little more flour until there are no cracks in it. Shape into two loaves. Place on a greased baking sheet. Let rise again for 15 minutes. Dip a pastry brush in milk and brush the top of the bread. Prick 5 holes in each loaf to let the air bubbles out. Bake at 350° F. for about an hour.

Not much wheat is grown in Norway. It has to be imported and is therefore expensive, but rye is grown widely. Rye flour contains very little gluten, so a bread made with all rye flour will be very heavy and dense. Substituting 1 or 2 cups of white flour will result in a lighter loaf.

Lefse

Rolled-up *Flatbrød*
"Ja da!"

3 cups riced potatoes (cooked
    without salt)
1 tablespoon melted shortening
¾ cup flour
1 teaspoon sugar
1 teaspoon salt
    butter for spreading
    sugar for sprinkling

Measure riced potatoes into a bowl. Add melted shortening. Sift the flour, sugar and salt together and add to the potato mixture. Mix well. Form the dough into egg-sized balls. Roll out very thin on a lightly floured pastry cloth using a grooved rolling pin if you have one. Bake on a hot greased griddle until bubbles form on top. Turn and brown on other side. It should be moist and pliable after it is baked.

Fold each cake in half, then in thirds until it looks like a flat cone. Stack them on a plate and keep a tea towel over them until serving time. Pass the plate at supper so that each person may spread his *lefse* with butter, sprinkle with sugar, or both.

Sigrid likes butter and goat cheese on hers. Erna remembers lefse *as a snack. Butter and sugar were put on the* lefse, *which was then rolled up like a cigar, and all the children walked around eating them.* Lefse *is good with coffee.*

The traditional lefse *of Norway is made of mashed potatoes, rye flour and water. We did not think this would appeal to Americans, so Sigrid got the delightful recipe of Mrs. Clarine Strand of Birmingham, a third generation Norwegian, who had sent her* lefse *at Christmas time.*

Flatbread

Flatbrød
Welcome at every meal.

2 cups rolled oats
1½ cups whole wheat flour
½ cup white flour
2 tablespoons sugar
½ teaspoon salt
1½ cups water
½ cup melted butter

Put the dry rolled oats into the blender. Blend, and it will become flour in a few minutes. Sift with the other flours, sugar and salt into a bowl and mix in the water and melted butter with a pastry blender to make a nice smooth dough. Chill.

The *flatbrød* will be very thin, so use a canvas-covered board or plastic pastry sheet and a stockinet-covered rolling pin. Flour board and pin slightly. Grease a cookie sheet. Roll out a piece of dough to fit it. Since you might tear the thin dough while lifting it to the pan, roll it up on the pin and roll it out onto the pan. Trim hang-over edges.

If you have a *riflet-kjevle* this is the time to roll it over the dough to make a pattern of holes. If not, prick dough with a fork. Mark the dough into cracker-sized pieces. Bake at 350° F. for about 10 minutes. If you put the pan on the bottom rack first, then shift it to the top rack, it will acquire a nice tan without burning.

Of course, if you have a big round special griddle as they do in Norway, you may bake it on this, turning the *flatbrød* with two long spatulas to bake on the other side. Since it will come off the stove large and round, it will have to be broken into smaller pieces for serving.

In Norway, Thorild Andreasdatter Bøe, Erna's grandmother, would have a special woman come in to help bake up the winter's supply of flatbrød. *It was then stacked like great phonograph records in the rat-proof* stabbur, *the food building.*

White Bread
Loff

2½ cups milk, divided
2 packages dry yeast
1 tablespoon sugar
4 cups white flour, divided
2 cups rye flour
1 teaspoon salt

Bring milk to a boil and cool to luke-warm. Place ½ cup of it in a big bowl; stir in the yeast and sugar and 1 tablespoon of the white flour. Let it bubble and rise in a warm place for 15 minutes. Sift the white and rye flours together; add the salt, and stir into the remaining 2 cups of lukewarm milk. Work to a fine dough. Then add the yeast mixture and stir well. Turn out on a floured board and knead for 15 minutes.

Grease and flour two loaf pans. Shape the dough into two pretty loaves, place them in the pans and let rise for 1 hour in a warm place. Preheat oven to 350° F. and bake the loaves for about 1 hour.

This is a special bread for Sunday morning to eat with your eggs. For other meals it is often served buttered with soup.

Potato Cakes
Poteteskake

1 cup white flour
1 cup rye flour
½ teaspoon salt
2 cups boiled and mashed potatoes, cooled

Sift the flours and salt together and mix with the mashed potatoes to a smooth dough. Roll out saucer-sized cakes, knife thin. If they are thick in the middle and humpy, they will not cook properly.

Put the griddle on slow heat and grease it. Cook cakes until brown on the bottom, turn over and brown on the other side.

Serve with butter, sugar and honey, or Norwegian goat cheese, if you can get it. A mild cheddar cheese will do.

If you go to a kaffe-stove *(coffee house) in the afternoon, you will get* poteteskake, vaffler, *or* lefse.

Sour Cream Waffles
Vaffler

2 cups sour cream
2 eggs
1 cup flour
1 teaspoon baking powder
½ teaspoon baking soda
½ teaspoon salt
2 tablespoons sugar
½ teaspoon ground cardamom
2 tablespoons water

Beat sour cream with egg beater until fluffy. In a separate bowl, beat the eggs until light. Combine with cream and beat again. Sift together the dry ingredients and fold gently into the sour cream and egg mixture. Add the water.

Grease a medium-hot waffle iron and bake the waffles until golden brown. If you must wait to serve them, put them on a rack on a pan in the oven and keep warm. Makes about 12. There won't be a crumb left.

It was such fun for Erna to bake waffles for John Xan. He always ordered a dozen, and ate them one at a time, filling each little square hole with maple syrup before he began.

Everyday Pancakes
Almindelige Pannekaker

4 eggs
1 quart milk (or buttermilk)
4 cups flour
½ teaspoon salt
margarine for frying

Beat eggs well. Add milk and flour alternately. (If buttermilk is used, add ½ teaspoon baking soda to the flour.) Add the salt. Stir until smooth. In a large skillet, melt margarine for each panful of batter. Spoon batter in and cook until cakes are firm enough to turn. Flip cakes over and brown on the other side. Keep cakes warm in a large covered bowl until mealtime. Serves 6.

Pea or vegetable soup was a first course, followed by these pancakes. This was Henning's Saturday night menu all his life. If Sigrid changed it, he grumbled and so did the dog. "Tjafs," their little terrier, knew when Saturday came. All day he sat beside the kitchen door, knowing that the last pancake after supper would be his. (Tjafs was named after a famous comic strip dog in Norway.)

Hearty Pork Pancakes
Fleskepannekaker
For a working man.

4 to 6 strips salt pork (streak of fat, streak of lean)
batter from Everyday Pancakes
2 tablespoons chopped chives

Cut rind off pork. Place pork in boiling water in a large skillet. Boil 3 minutes to extract the salt. Pour the water off. Fry the pork in the skillet until light brown. Pour off most of the grease. Arrange the pork in the skillet in serving sections. Cover all carefully with Everyday Pancake batter. Sprinkle with chives. Cook over low heat until it is firm all the way through. Does not have to be turned. When serving, cut into individual pieces.

Believe it or not, Sigrid insists that for supper Norwegians eat a buttered slice of bread with this, and nothing else except a cup of hot coffee. Although they eat it for supper, here in America it would make a nice luncheon dish.

Finer Pancakes
Finere Pannekaker
For dessert.

6 eggs
1 cup half-and-half cream
4 tablespoons flour
1 cup milk
½ teaspoon salt
1 teaspoon sugar
margarine for frying
sugar and/or jam

Beat eggs until they foam. Add the cream and stir in the flour until smooth. Add milk, salt and sugar. Let stand for two hours "so the flour can expand," as they say in Norway.

Use an 8-inch skillet. Pancakes are much easier to handle in a small skillet. Grease skillet with margarine before making each pancake. Put just enough batter in to cover the bottom. Pancakes must be thin. Cook over very low heat. When they are firm enough to turn, do so, and let the other side cook until light brown. Keep warm in a covered bowl until dessert time. Serve with sugar and/or jam. Makes about 16.

Norwegian utensils for bakkels (pastries) at Vesterheim, the Norwegian-American Museum, Decorah, Iowa. Egg waffles (eaten cold), goro (a thin rectangular shortbread) and krumkaker (a crisp round egg wafer shaped as a cone) were standard pastries which needed special irons. Originally these had long handles for use on the open fire. Later they were adapted to fit the round openings of a range. Rosettes (crisp lacy cakes fried in deep fat) are now made on cast iron or aluminum irons. Fattigmann needs no special irons. These cakes were made from rolled-out dough cut into diamonds and fried in deep fat. The supply of pastries baked at Christmas usually lasted until spring. *Photograph by Joan Liffring-Zug.*

34

Cakes, Cookies and Desserts

Duchess Cake

Hertuginnekake

This is Sigrid's birthday cake.

6 large eggs
1 cup sifted sugar
1½ cups sifted flour
½ teaspoon baking powder

Let your mixer do the work! Beat eggs in large bowl until light and lemon-colored. Gradually add the sugar and let the mixer work at medium speed for 30 minutes. Sift flour and baking powder together. Remove bowl from mixer and begin sifting the flour mixture over the dough, gently folding over and over with a spoon until all flour is incorporated.

Grease bottom of a tube pan, then cut a circle of waxed paper to fit the bottom (hole cut out). Place waxed paper in pan and grease the paper. Dust the whole pan with flour. Carefully spoon in the dough and smooth the top to make it level. Bake at 325° F. for 50 minutes. It should shrink slightly away from the sides of the pan when done. Invert pan to cool, then remove the cake to a cake rack.

Cut in three even layers, using tooth-picks for guides. Place bottom layer on a cake plate and cover with half the filling. Put the second layer on and use remainder of filling. Place the top layer on and glaze the cake. When glazing is dry (you might put it in the refrigerator for a while), decorate the cake in a fancy way.

Filling:
2 cups whipping cream
2 tablespoons sugar
1 cup finely chopped blanched almonds
½ teaspoon vanilla

Whip cream stiffly, add sugar, and fold in almonds and vanilla. Use this to spread between layers of cake.

Glaze:
1 cup confectioners' sugar
2 tablespoons cold water
½ teaspoon lemon juice

Mix all ingredients together well and spread on top of cake with a knife that is dipped repeatedly in warm water.

Cake Decoration:
1 cup stiffly whipped cream (one 5½-ounce carton of Cool Whip will do)

Fill decorator tube half full, use a fancy tip and make a wreath around the cake. Put pretty little mounds in the middle.

In summer, decorate with fresh raspberries or strawberries; in winter, crystallized fruit. Once you get a decorating tube in your hand, there will be no stopping you and you can let your imagination run wild. But it all spells "Happy Birthday!" to your own "Duchess" or "Duke."

Prince's Cake
Fyrstekake

1 cup flour
½ cup sugar
1 teaspoon baking powder
½ cup butter
1 egg
1 teaspoon almond extract

Sift flour, sugar and baking powder and add to butter as for making pastry. Add whole egg and almond extract and knead well. Cut the dough in two. One part is rolled out to a ¼-inch thickness in a round shape. Place it on a greased baking sheet.

Filling:
½ cup unblanched almonds
⅔ cup confectioners' sugar
¼ teaspoon cinnamon
¼ teaspoon ground cardamom
3 tablespoons water
1 egg white

Leave skin on almonds. Wipe them clean between wet cloths. Grind them once in a meat grinder until they look like small grains. Sift confectioners' sugar with spices and add to the almonds. Add water and stir to a heavy paste. Now, spread this paste on the rolled-out dough to within ¼ inch of the edge.

Roll out the other half of the dough to "half the thickness of the little finger" (about ¼ inch thick) and cut with a knife into strips ½ inch wide. (It is pretty if these are cut with a pinked-edge cutter.) Weave the strips in and out like lattice-work over the filling. Leftover pieces of dough are made into a ¾-inch thick ring that goes all the way around the edge of the cake. Beat egg white slightly and brush it all over the pastry on top of the cake. Bake at 350° F. for 25 minutes. Serves 6.

This is a cake fit for a prince, but nobody knows which Prince it was named after. So in 1974 Sigrid and Erna dedicated theirs to Norway's newest infant Prince Haakon Magnus, son of Crown Prince Harald and Crown Princess Sonja.

Potato Torte
Fin Potetkake
For coffees or teas.

½ cup hot mashed potatoes
5 tablespoons butter
½ cup sugar
1 cup uncooked rolled oats
12 drops almond extract

Put potatoes in a mixing bowl; add in succession the butter, sugar, oats and almond extract. Stir until well mixed. On a greased cookie sheet spread the dough out the size and shape of a dinner plate. Bake at 325° F. until light brown. Take it from the oven, cool, and then glaze it. Makes about 12 pieces.

Glaze:
Flormelis Glasur
2 cups confectioners' sugar
3 tablespoons boiling water
1 teaspoon vanilla

Mix well so glaze will spread easily. Cover the top of the torte.
When you serve this deilig (delicious) potetkake, nobody ever dreams what is in it, the common potato.

Cream Puff Pretzel
Vandbakkelskringle

1 cup water
½ cup butter
1 cup flour
4 eggs

Boil water and butter in a saucepan until butter is melted. Remove from heat and add flour all at once. Stir quickly, put back on heat and stir until it forms a ball. Beat in the eggs one at a time. Remove from heat and cool slightly.

Preheat oven to exactly 425° F. Grease baking sheet and spoon the mixture by tablespoonfuls to make the shape of a big pretzel. Bake for 20 minutes, then turn heat down to 325° and bake for 15 minutes more. At the end of this time, pinch pretzel gently to see if it is firm. If not, let it bake another 5 minutes. Don't overbake. Cool it on the tin and ice the top, then remove it to a serving plate. Serves about 14.

Icing:
1½ cups confectioners' sugar
    a little water to make a paste
1 teaspoon vanilla

Mix ingredients together and drizzle over the pretzel. Each serving gets about 1 tablespoon icing.
This is elegant with coffee or tea.

Cream Patches
Fløtelapper

3 eggs, beaten
1 pint half-and-half cream
5 tablespoons flour
1 tablespoon sugar
¼ teaspoon salt
¼ teaspoon ground cardamom
    margarine for frying
    sugar, syrup or jam for topping

Beat the eggs until foamy. Add half-and-half alternately with the flour and beat until smooth. Then add sugar, salt and cardamom. Melt margarine in large skillet. Drop dough by tablespoonfuls and cook until firm, then turn over and cook the other side to light brown. (They should be about the shape of patches on a pair of pants; this is where they get their name.)

Keep them warm in a covered dish till served. At the table, top them with sugar, syrup or jam. Serves about 6.

In Sigrid's childhood, syrup came in little kegs with a spigot. One went to the Kolonial Butikk (grocery) with one's own little bucket or pitcher and bought as much as it would hold. Wheat, sugar and spices were also imported and sold at the Kolonial.

'World's Best' Syrup Cookies
Sirupskaker-"Verdens Beste"

1 cup margarine
1 cup sugar
½ cup light corn syrup
2 tablespoons water
4 cups flour
½ teaspoon baking soda
2 teaspoons cinnamon
½ teaspoon ground cloves

In a small saucepan heat the margarine, sugar and syrup. After it is warmed, add the water. Cool. Sift flour, baking soda and spices and stir into the syrup mixture. Shape the dough into two long rolls about 2 inches in diameter. Wrap each roll in waxed paper and store in refrigerator overnight.

The next day, remove waxed paper and cut roll in thin slices and place on greased cookie sheet. Bake at 375° F. about 10 minutes or until done. Makes over 100 cookies.

Cornucopias

Kremmerhus

¾ cup plus 2 tablespoons butter
¾ cup sugar
1¾ cups flour
1 teaspoon vanilla
6 egg whites

Cream the butter and sugar until light and lemon-colored. Stir in the flour and vanilla. Beat egg whites until very stiff. Fold the egg whites gently into the butter mixture. Grease a Teflon baking sheet and drop the dough by teaspoonfuls onto it. With a long knife, flatten them out to thin rounds of even thickness all the way across. (If the edges are too thin, they will crack in the rolling. If the middles are too thick, they will crack.) Bake at 300°F. until light tan, about 10 minutes.

Open the oven, but do not take the cookies out. Remove one cookie at a time with a spatula, and quickly roll over a wooden spoon handle, or better, a cone-shaped wooden *Kremmerhusform*. If the cookie gets brittle, put it back in the oven for a few minutes, and you can roll it again. They stiffen almost instantly out of the oven. Makes about 60.

Filling:
 Cool Whip or other whipped
  topping
 strawberry jam

Just before serving, mix Cool Whip and strawberry jam and stuff some in each cornucopia. You will have instant fame as a gourmet cook!

Teflon and Cool Whip may not have been found in the early Norwegian kitchen, but they are convenient substitutes for an iron griddle and whipped cream.

Butter Rings

Smørkranser

2 eggs
1 cup sugar
2 tablespoons finely chopped
  blanched almonds
1 teaspoon vanilla
4 cups flour
1½ cups butter or margarine

Beat eggs and sugar until light and lemon-colored. Add chopped almonds and vanilla. With hands, add flour and butter alternately until dough is smooth. Put into a cookie press with small star-shaped opening. Press out a long length and then cut into 4-inch pieces. Turn each piece into a circle. Place on a greased cookie sheet and bake at 375°F. for 10 to 12 minutes or until light tan. Makes about 120.

This is a good standby cookie the year around.

Oatmeal Macaroons

Havremakroner

1 cup melted butter or margarine
1 cup sugar
1 egg, beaten
4 tablespoons cream
½ teaspoon almond extract
1 cup flour
1 teaspoon baking powder
2½ cups rolled oats

Mix butter and sugar until fluffy. Add beaten egg, then the cream and almond extract. Beat well. Sift flour and baking powder. Add this to the butter mixture and beat again. Stir in the oats and mix well. Place by teaspoonfuls on a greased baking sheet. Bake at 250°F. for 20 minutes or until dry and crisp. Makes about 75 cookies.

Everybody asks for this recipe. It is easy, cheap and delicious.

Berlin Wreaths
Berlinerkranser

4 hard-cooked egg yolks, cooled
4 raw egg yolks
1 cup plus 2 tablespoons sugar
4 cups flour
2¼ cups sweet butter

Mash the four hard-cooked egg yolks and mix with the four raw yolks until smooth. Add the sugar and beat well. Alternately add the flour and butter and knead until smooth. Chill for 1 hour.

To make cookies, pinch off a lump of dough and roll on a canvas-covered, lightly floured board to thickness of a little finger. Cut into 5-inch lengths. Cross ends over to make a wreath.

Topping:
4 slightly beaten egg whites
½ pound sugar lumps, coarsely crushed

Dip cookies into egg white and sprinkle with coarsely crushed sugar. Lay on a greased cookie sheet and bake at 375°F. until lightly tan, about 10 to 12 minutes. Makes about 125.

Everybody in Norway makes these cookies for Christmas. They melt in the mouth. Those with the most sugar on them always get eaten first, they are so good and crunchy. Jon Rolf Marstrander, Sigrid's grandson, calls his favorite cookies "The Crossovers."

Stacked Cookies
Bordstabelbakkels

2 eggs
2 tablespoons cream
1 cup sugar
4 cups flour, sifted
2 cups sweet butter or margarine, melted

Beat eggs, cream and sugar until light and lemon-colored. Add flour and butter alternately. Chill. Roll very thin and cut into long strips 1 inch wide. Bake on a greased cookie sheet at 350°F. until very light tan. Check at 10 minutes. Take from oven and cut into 4-inch lengths while still warm. Ice as follows. Makes about 120 cookies.

Icing:
3 egg whites
1 cup confectioners' sugar
1 cup hazelnuts, blanched and chopped

Beat egg whites to a stiff peak. Add confectioners' sugar gradually, then fold in the nuts. In the middle of each cookie, lay a strip of frosting decoration. Put the cookies back into the oven at 200° and dry the frosting. Remove when dry.

To serve, lay a paper doily on a plate and stack the cookie strips like lumber in a three-cornered hollow tower. Makes a very pretty center for the table.

Children's Cookies
Pleskener

2 eggs
2 egg yolks
1 cup sugar
1½ cups flour
¾ cup cornstarch
1 teaspoon vanilla
    candied citron, finely chopped

Beat eggs and yolks with the sugar until light and lemon-colored. Sift together flour and cornstarch and stir into the egg mixture. Add vanilla. Grease a cookie sheet and drop the dough by teaspoonfuls. Place a little citron in the middle of each. Bake at 325°F. until light tan. Makes about 75.

Sand Cakes

Sandkaker

A luncheon dessert in tartlet cups.

1 cup butter or margarine
1 cup confectioners' sugar
1 egg
2 cups sifted flour
½ cup blanched ground almonds

Cream butter, add sugar and stir until lemon-colored. Add egg and beat well. Add sifted flour and ground almonds. Butter tartlet tins (small round tins with ruffled edges) and press dough to inside, just to the rim. Bake at 350°F. for about 12 minutes or until light golden brown. Cool slightly and invert them to remove pastry cups from tins. Do not fill until just before serving time or they will become soggy. Makes about 60.

Filling:
1 pint whipping cream
1 tablespoon sugar
¼ teaspoon almond extract
strawberry or raspberry jam for decoration

Combine first three ingredients and beat until stiff. At dessert time fill tartlet cups with whipped cream mixture, and place a half teaspoon of red jam on top.

These tartlets are delicious eaten just as a cookie, without being filled.

Peasant Girls with Veils

Tilslørtebondepiker

¼ cup butter
2 cups finely crushed zwieback
1 tablespoon sugar
½ teaspoon cinnamon
1 cup jam or applesauce
1 cup whipped cream, sweetened to taste

Melt butter in a skillet over low heat. Add the zwieback mixed with sugar and cinnamon and stir until light brown. Cool. In a dessert bowl, alternate three layers of zwieback mixture and two layers of jam or applesauce and cream. Top with whipped cream. Serves 4 or 5.

Nobody could tell us where this dish got its fancy name, but it appears just like this in 75-year-old cookbooks. When one sees it, though, in a sparkling cut-glass bowl adorned with whipped cream and ladled out with an elegant sterling silver spoon, it really is "all dressed up."

Prune Compote

Sviskekompot

12 ounces pitted dried prunes
1 tablespoon sugar
¼ cup apple or orange juice
2 tablespoons cornstarch
⅓ cup water
1 cup prune juice
whipped cream, with sugar and vanilla to taste

Wash prunes. Soak them overnight in about a quart of water.

Next morning, boil in a covered kettle for ½ hour. Take them up with a slotted spoon and save the juice. When prunes are cool, put them into a serving dish.

Strain the juice and put one cupful into a small saucepan. Add sugar and apple or orange juice. Bring to a boil. Stir the cornstarch into the ⅓ cup water and add to the juice in the pan. Bring to a boil again, stirring constantly. Take off the stove and, when slightly cool, pour over the prunes in the dish. Serve with whipped cream on top.

Apricot Compote
Aprikoskompot

12 ounces dried apricots
2 tablespoons sugar
   sweetened whipped cream or
   half-and-half cream

Wash apricots. Soak in water to cover overnight.

Next morning, add sugar and cook slowly until they are mushy. Cool and spoon into individual dishes. Serve with sweetened whipped cream or half-and-half.

Eggedosis
Eggedosis
For desserts and receptions.

5 egg yolks
10 teaspoons sugar
1 egg white, stiffly beaten

Beat egg yolks and sugar until thick and lemon-colored. This will take a long time; an electric mixer can be used. Fold in stiffly beaten egg white. Serve in punch cups and eat with a spoon. Serves 5.

This is a traditional treat on the 17th of May, Norway's "Fourth of July." It's rich and delicious; you will remember its taste forever. Any number can be served if you use 1 egg yolk and 2 teaspoons sugar per person. Serve dainty cookies with it.

Red Berry Pudding with Cream
Rødgrøt med Fløte

If you can say this, you can speak Norwegian.

1 10-ounce box frozen strawberries
1 10-ounce box frozen raspberries
   as much water as berries and juice
   whipped cream, Cool Whip or half-
   and-half cream
5 tablespoons cornstarch
5 tablespoons sugar

Place berries and water in a saucepan and cook for 5 minutes. Strain through a sieve. This should make about 4½ cups juice. Mix the cornstarch and sugar and add water to make a thin paste. Bring the juice again to a boil. Take off the heat and stir in the cornstarch mixture. Bring it back to a boil quickly, and after 2 minutes take it off the stove. Cool it a little before you pour it carefully into a glass bowl or individual serving dishes. (Don't crack the dishes!) To prevent a skin from forming, sprinkle a little sugar on top of each dish.

Rødgrøt is better if made several hours ahead or the day before serving. At dessert time, top with whipped cream, Cool Whip or half-and-half cream. Serves 6.

This is Norway's National Dessert. It can be made with fresh currants or blackberries, or canned wild blueberries or blackberries. Just be sure you have 4½ cups juice after putting the berries through the sieve.

Tray doily in satin and chain stitch embroidery has the inscription "Kaffe gi'r Humør" (Coffee makes the spirits bright). Vesterheim collection.

41

Rice Cream

Riskrem

Best made a day ahead.

2¼ cups milk
¼ cup rice
1½ tablespoons sugar
4 tablespoons blanched and chopped almonds
2 tablespoons butter
1 pint whipping cream, whipped stiff
1 teaspoon vanilla
1 envelope unflavored gelatin
½ cup cold water

Put milk in top of double boiler and bring to a boil. When it is bubbling around the edge, add the rice and stir. Let cook for about 50 minutes or until rice is well done. While still hot, add sugar, almonds, and butter. Let it cool completely.

Fold in the stiffly beaten whipped cream and the vanilla. Sprinkle gelatin over cold water in a small saucepan. Place over low heat, stirring constantly until gelatin dissolves (about 3 minutes). Cool. Fold into the rice and whipped cream mixture. Spoon into a big pretty bowl and refrigerate. Serves 8.

Red Sauce:
1 box frozen strawberries
1 cup water
1½ tablespoons cornstarch

Boil strawberries and water for 5 minutes. Dissolve cornstarch in a little water. Add to the sauce, bring to a boil stirring constantly. Remove from heat, and cool.

When serving, pass the bowl of rice cream around the table followed by a pitcher of the red sauce to pour over the rice.

Caramel Pudding

Karamelpudding

Glaze:
1¼ cups granulated sugar
1½ cups water

Put sugar and water in an iron or other heavy skillet. Boil until it gets dry and starts to melt and become golden brown. Pour it immediately into a dry round or oblong mold and turn mold around quickly until glaze entirely covers the sides and bottom of the mold. Keep turning until glaze stiffens.

Custard:
5 egg yolks
3 egg whites
3 tablespoons sugar
1 pint half-and-half cream
½ cup milk
1 teaspoon vanilla

Preheat oven to 325° F. Beat egg yolks and whites with the sugar until light and lemon-colored. In a small saucepan bring cream and milk to boil; remove from heat and add vanilla. Pour it slowly over the egg mixture, beating constantly. Cool completely and pour it into the mold.

Now, place the mold in a pan with water halfway up the mold's sides. Bake for 1½ hours. The water must be kept at the boiling point all the time. If it evaporates, add more boiling water to the pan. Take pudding out of the oven and let cool. When cold, invert the custard on a plate with an edge to keep the glaze from running off. Serves 4 or 5.

This dish is best made as much as a day ahead of time and kept chilled. You wouldn't be ashamed to serve it to a Queen or a President's wife.

Apple Pie

As American as "Mom." My "Mom" was born on December 27, 1866, at Winchester, Wisconsin, six months after her parents arrived in this country and was their first American.   *—E.O.X.*

Pastry for 9" double crust:
- ½ **cup corn oil**
- ¼ **cup cold milk**
- 2 **cups sifted flour**
- 1 **teaspoon salt**

Combine the corn oil and milk together in a measuring cup. Mix flour and salt in a bowl. Dig a little hole and dump oil and milk into it. Stir lightly with a fork until well-blended and dough "cleans" the sides of the bowl. Press into a smooth ball and divide, making one part a little bigger.

Tear off four 12-inch squares of waxed paper. Wipe tabletop with damp cloth to keep waxed paper from slipping. Place smaller ball between two papers and, with a rolling pin, roll dough out into a 12-inch circle. Discard top waxed paper. Lift bottom paper and crust and lay it upside-down in pie pan. While peeling paper away, pat crust into place, leaving no bubbles beneath. Handle as little as possible. Trim edges a little bigger than rim of pan.

Roll out upper crust in the same way. Remove top paper. With a knife tip, cut a leaf design in it like "Mom" used to make (shown below). Let top crust remain on the paper while you prepare the filling.

Filling:
- 6 **or 7 cups peeled, cored and sliced tart, juicy apples**
- ¾ **cup sugar**
- ¼ **cup flour**
- **dash of salt**
- ¼ **teaspoon nutmeg**
- ¼ **teaspoon cinnamon**
- 2 **tablespoons butter**

Combine sugar, flour, salt and spices; sprinkle over apples and stir gently. Heap into bottom crust. Dot with butter.

Lift waxed paper and top crust and flop crust over the apples. Discard paper. Trim crust about ½ inch bigger than bottom crust and tuck extra dough under rim of bottom crust. Press rim all around with tines of a fork, or flute with your fingers. This will keep the juice from running over into the oven. Bake at 450°F. for 10 minutes, then at 350° for 35 to 40 minutes more, until crust is golden brown and juice is bubbling through the decoration.

Serve with wedges of yellow cheese.

Apple Pie in Norway

By Erna Oleson Xan

One of the most elegant homes I visited in Norway was the Neri Valen estate in Bø, Telemark. (All my grandparents had been born in Telemark, too, and emigrated to the same district in Wisconsin during the mid-1800's. Telemark was like home.) I can see the Valen place now, on a hill, the tall, broad, white, twenty-four-room house surrounded by green trees, with a rose-garden in its lap. High on the right side, the red-blue-and-white Norwegian flag flung out its welcome in the stiff breeze.

Mistress of the house was Ingebjørg Vaa Valen, whose late husband, Neri, had been a member of Parliament and a hero of World War II. She was also a sister of Hjørdis, wife of my cousin, Olav Bøe. They were my hosts in this summer of 1955.

"What do you raise on your land?" I asked Ingebjorg as we sat around the coffee table.

"Oh," she replied, "cattle, and hundreds of apple trees."

"Apples," I cried. "Think of the pies you must eat!"

Pie? The company looked at each other. They had *heard* of pie. Ingebjørg remembered pie when she went with her young husband to America thirty years earlier.

Then all eyes turned on me. Would Erna make them a pie? Oh, I was a pie-baker from 'way back! So we proceeded to the summer kitchen.

I told them I would need a few things—measuring cups and spoons, pie tins, shortening, apples, sugar. Instead, Ingebjørg's daughter, Marit Lie, brought me a gram-scale. They didn't have measuring spoons and cups. Would a big coffee cup do?

The flour was yellow Hungarian wheat; the shortening, margarine made of whale oil. How many grams would I need? I hoped Marit did not see my red face. What on earth was I into? I had not seen a 'gram' since I left college.

Marit went for some spices and salt and a big pan of apples. As she was building up a good fire in the kitchen stove, I said all I needed was some bowls, and could do the rest alone. (I did not want her to watch me 'shame the family name.')

The apples were big and tart and juicy. I peeled and sliced them very thin, doused them with a mixture of flour, sugar, cinnamon and nutmeg. A little salt. Tasting it over and over with trembling tongue.

Then, gingerly, I mixed a large white cup of margarine, two-and-a-half cups of yellow flour, and a little more salt. To make the dough tender and mixed, I used two knives, slipping and cutting past each other till it resembled crumbs. Now and then a little sprinkle of water to make it stick. I was afraid it would be as tough as leather. After rolling it out, I flung it on the tin, patted it to fit and piled it high with apples. (By now the crackling of the eager stove made me sweat for more reasons than one.)

I scraped some hunks of butter over the apples, made doughstrips for criss-crossing on top, sealed and crimped the edges with fumbling hands. There were lots of scraps of dough left over for children's pies.

Now for the oven! I stared hard at the figures on the door's temperature dial. It was Greek to me—"Celsius." Calling Marit, I asked what did that add up to in "Fahrenheit." She looked at me—what was "Fahrenheit?"

At this, I placed a piece of white paper on the oven rack. As soon as it turned tan, I popped in the pie and shut the door.

Now, the waiting and the awful truth! If I hadn't been a home economics major in college . . . why hadn't I kept my big mouth shut about pie?

As I was making little pies for the children, I smelled something and flung open the oven door. The side of the crust nearest the fire-box was browning too fast. I turned it around. Soon the other side darkened. I turned it a little more and laid a piece of paper on it.

But something wonderful was happening! The kitchen was filling with the heavenly aroma of apples-and-sugar-and-cinnamon. The pie was bubbling through the lattice-work; yes, even trickling over the side onto the oven floor. Those Telemark Apples were doing their duty for me, a "Telemark *Pike*" (girl) from 'way back!

The pie was done! It was a little lopsided, a little too brown on the edges, but the scraps had told me the crust was crumbly-crisp.

By dinner-time dessert, oh, what an eager circle of beloved faces watched Ingebjørg bear that big pie to my place. One by one, I counted with the knife in air. There were Ingebjørg, Anna, Sverre, Marit, and Halvor, Olav, Hjørdis, Erna. There was plenty to go around, and the children were squealing over their pies.

The hostess passed a plate of yellow cheese. Hey Hopp! Giddy with success, I sang out:

"Apple pie without the cheese
Is like the kiss without the squeeze!"

They were all so crazy over that pie that I had to promise to send them recipes when I got home . . . And I added three sets of American measuring cups and spoons, pastry-flakers and pie-pans. Marit Lie became the famous pie expert of Bø, Telemark.

And that is how Erna Oleson Xan, third generation, thoroughbred Norwegian-American, brought Apple Pie to *Gamle Norge.**

*"Old Norway". An affectionate name for their Homeland.

This porcelain bowl in the form of a benign dragon is from the Porcelain Factory in Norway. Vesterheim collection.

From The
The Vesterheim Collection

Sour-cream porridge (rømme-grøt) was often carried to feasts, and the wealth of the farm from where it came was reflected in the ornateness of the container. Gudbrandsdalen, where this piece originated, became the center for massive wood porridge containers heavily carved with acanthus scrolls picked up by the rural craftmen of the area from the baroque art in upper-class homes.

Acanthus carving found its way to almost every wood object in Gudbrandsdalen. This oval box with a snap-on cover is called a "tine" (pronounced teené) and was used to carry food or articles of clothing while traveling or making the long trek to church.

Top: Copper was mined in east-central Norway, and from about 1750 it replaced iron and stone for cooking utensils and wood for dippers. One of this type often hung on the edge of a copper cooler at the door of east Norwegian homes. A visitor was expected to take from it as a sign of being friendly to the house.

Vesterheim Collection

Below: Pastry cutters of wood carved to make a toothed edge were used largely for "fattigmann" (poor man's cakes), a crisp rag-like pastry made of milk, eggs, sugar, and flour, rolled out, cut in diamonds, and fried in deep fat.

Below, right: Beer was brought from the storehouse to the table in large stave-constructed tankards and poured into bowls from which everyone drank. Many such bowls, like the one in the illustration, had animal heads to serve as handles. This type of design goes back to the Viking age and is seen in the ships of that time.

Not only objects for the table were decorated. The mangle boards used with a roller to work the wrinkles out of newly washed linen are show-pieces of the carver's art. Many were made as betrothal gifts and had to please the maiden being courted. The illustrated example from 1800 was by one of Norway's most famous carvers, Christen Listad of Gudbrandsdalen.

Above left: "Tine" boxes could be plain, carved, or decorated with rose-maling like this one. Its somewhat small size and pastel rococo decoration indicates that it might have been used for a woman's special things rather than for lunches or clothes. It could have carried her knitting or embroidery materials.

Above right: Beer bowls were often decorated because they were used largely for festive occasions. Examples with acanthus carving on the outside and rosemaling on the inside are rare but are found in Valdres, the area from which this one came. Writing the inscription upside-down around the interior edge of the bowl is also typical for the area.

Bottom right: Before soap and washing machines, clothes in Norway were washed by being boiled and pounded on rocks so that the dirt would be forced out with the water. Paddles for this purpose were often plain, but geometric chip carving on the back, as seen here, was not uncommon.

Left: Butter was special to the Norwegians and was served on festive occasions in fancy tubs with carving inside the cover to leave a decorative impression on the golden surface.

A large block of Geitost *(goat cheese)* *is shown on a table cloth from Norway* *with Norwegian candlesticks at the* *home of Sigrid Marstrander. The bread* *is Norwegian rye bread. Flowers are* *camellias.* Photographs by Darrell Henning.

Caramel pudding; the recipe is on *page 42.*

49

Norway. Vesterheim photograph by Dean Madden.

Norway. *Vesterheim photograph by Dean Madden.*
Below: Lake Miøsa, Hamar, Norway. *Photograph by Darrell Henning.*

Norway

Stave Church, Nesbyen, Norway.

- Norway ranks sixth in quantities of fish taken from the sea.
- Norway's coast is 15,000 miles long.
- By 1900, a total of 900,000 Norwegians had emigrated to America, a number greater than the population of Norway.
* In Tromsø the sun never sets from May 20 to July 23.
* Norway is as far north as Alaska, but is warmer because of the Gulf Stream.
- Since 1905, when Norway gained freedom from Sweden, the King's right to veto legislation has never been used.
- Norway has 150,000 lakes and 50,000 islands.
- The map of Norway has been likened to a giant fish, its tail in the north, its mouth in the south (Oslo).

Hallingdahl, Norway. Photography by Darrell Henning.

Lake Miøsa, Hamar, Norway. Photograph by Darrell Henning.

Norway in America

Norsk I Amerika

Photograph by Darrell Henning, Curator, Vesterheim

Above: One of the exhibitions in Norway presented images and patterns made by Norwegian-Americans and others influenced by them. The exhibitions were sponsored by Vesterheim, the Norwegian-American Museum, and coordinated by Norsk Utvandrermuseum (The Norwegian Emigrant Museum) in Norway in 1989.

The exhibitions included folk and decorative arts before and after 1970, paintings and drawings, and the photography of Andrew Dahl, a collection of late 19th-century photographs.

The embroidered wall hangings at left depict the departure from Norway and Minneapolis. Both pieces are from Vesterheim. Works by more than 100 craftsmen and fine artists were included in the exhibition.

the Evang farm at Toten. The jewelry was in a burial mound dating from 1100-1300 B.C. The plaid in the vest, purse and shawl are taken from a museum in Toten. The motifs for the Toten costume were developed within the last 10 years. The coverlet on the wall is from Sogn and hangs under a border of chalk painting on the upper log of the wall, done especially for the Christmas season. This ancient style of decoration was a forerunner of the more luxurious rosemaling.

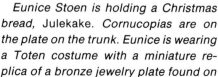

Eunice Stoen is holding a Christmas bread, Julekake. Cornucopias are on the plate on the trunk. Eunice is wearing a Toten costume with a miniature replica of a bronze jewelry plate found on

Doris and Dennis Barnaal, their daughter Kari, and Rockne Cole wear Gudbrandsdal costumes in front of a corner hearth from Gudbrandsdal in the Norwegian house at Vesterheim. Cookies on the plate are Berlinerkranser.

Karen Tjostem, holding butter rings, is wearing a Sogn costume. She is in the Victorian foyer of the main building at Vesterheim. The richly carpeted room is dedicated to Walter E. Olson, whose floor coverings from the Olson Rug Company gave distinction to many Norwegian immigrant homes in the 1930's.

Nora Guttebo in her costume from Vågå, Gudbrandsdal, stands with her granddaughter Kristin Guttebo in front of an 18th-century cupboard from the same area. Mrs. Guttebo is holding a pie, Fin potekake.

56

Ruth Reitan, with children's cookies, wears an authentic costume of a Hardanger matron and stands in front of a tapestry-woven coverlet which is also typical of Hardanger design.

Helen Hendrickson, wearing a costume from Voss, stands in front of the log wall of a replica Norwegian house at Vesterheim.

Ethel Martinson, in her authentic Telemark costume, sits in a room from Setesdal decked with straw for the Christmas holidays at Vesterheim. The cupboard behind her stands on a bench filled with earth to serve as insulation along the wall. In front of her is the sheaf of grain put out for birds on Christmas Eve.

The Rev. Donald Berg and his wife Barbara are seated at the massive loom from Hadeland, Norway, in the guest room of the Norwegian house at Vesterheim. The coverlet and ceremonial towels over the windows are an ancient part of Christmas decoration in the inner valleys of Norway. The costumes are from Valdres. Mrs. Berg is holding sandbakkels.

Centralized motifs in rather flat colors are typical of rosemaling in Hallingdal. The Twin Cities of Minnesota have become an American center for painting in this style. The piece at left was decorated in the 1970s by Addie Pittelkow of St. Paul. It is in the style of rural Norwegian decorative artists of a century ago. Vesterheim collection.

This trunk was decorated by a painter from Hallingdal who was active in Voss. The box is of a Vest Agder type and carries the inscription "Jeg staar her til Tieneste for min eier. Gunil Tonetta Ols Datter Bu Lien 1885" *(I stand here at the service of my owner).*

Photographs at Vesterheim of Norwegian-Americans in costume and of the Vesterheim trunks and bowls are by Joan Liffring-Zug.

This bentwood box cover from the mid-1960s is by Agnes Rykken.

This early bowl, repainted about 1900 in Hallingdal, gives a warning to the guest: "Drik fra dig og til en anden; Lad den gaa tit saa Vaerker Panden" *(Drink from yourself to someone else; Let it happen too often and your head will ache).*

Betty Nelson in her costume from Torpo, Hallingdal, sits on an immigrant trunk from the same area. The painted log chair is from neighboring Ål in Hallingdal.

The trunk on the left is by Kjetil or Ivar Urdal from Vest Agder. The trunk at right is by Thomas Luraas of Telemark.

The large blue bowl (at left) with white trim has this inscription: "Drik min ven, Skjaenk igjen, Send det til min Naboe hen. LIS og SSD 1858" (Drink my friend, Pour up again, Send it on to my neighbor).

The bowl with the white rim and red and yellow decoration has the following inscription: "Jeg Er Liden Og Net; Drik af mig Saa Gjør Du Ret. BTDD 1837" (I am little and nice; Drink of me and you do the right thing).

The large bowl with lip (Trøys), carries this inscription: "Liv Rasmus datter, Ødden den Store Gud So Treet Planter han ogsaa frugten vande(r) See til du ikke bander" (Liv, the daughter of Rasmus on the farm Ødden; the great God who plants the tree also waters the fruit. Be careful not to swear).

The small bowl with the white rim (right) has the inscription: "Smak paa det jeg haver inde, drik saa ut det hver en taar" (Taste what I have inside, drink up every last drop).

Hanging Cupboard

Between the long table that dominated one wall of a traditional Norwegian interior and a bed built into the corner hung a cupboard that contained the things most precious to the lady of the house. This example may be decorated by the well-known Telemark painter Thomas Luraas. It was a gift from a Norwegian museum to the Norwegian-American people and is now part of the Luther College collection at Vesterheim.

Vesterheim collection photographs.

Top left: Ethel Kvalheim of Stoughton, Wisconsin, was one of the first American painters to reach Gold Medal status at the Vesterheim National Exhibitions.

Bottom left: This light and cheerful small chest dated 1864, from an area south of Bergen, represents the last style of rosemaling to develop in Norway.

Above right: With its prominent Lion of Norway, this 1905 ale tankard from Lesjaskogen may reflect the freedom Norway won from Sweden during that year.

Bridal Crown

With blue glass set in silver and gold, this one dates from the mid-18th century, probably made in Bergen. It is 10 inches in diameter. Brought to America by the family of Olaf Skaar of La Crosse, Wisconsin, it was presented to Vesterheim by his children.

The use of bridal crowns is a distinctively Scandinavian custom. It may have arisen from the practice during the Catholic period of adorning the image of the Madonna, Queen of Heaven, in the churches with an actual crown. The earliest extant bridal crowns are thought once to have served this purpose. The crown is a symbol of virginity and was worn by the bride through the early portion of the elaborate wedding celebrations held in the rural areas of Norway until recent times. It was owned by either the family or the church and remained in use from generation to generation. Several examples brought to America by immigrants have come to Vesterheim, but none excel in grandeur that of the Skaar family.

Bridal Procession in Sogn—Painting by Hans Dahl (c. 1890s)
This work was on loan to Vesterheim from Margaret Eckhardt during the centennial of the museum in 1977.

The Wedding in Norway

When the painting at left was on loan to Vesterheim, two museum visitors identified the bride and bridegroom. The visitors were Kjellaug Ese, a nurse at the Mayo Clinic, and her sister Anna. The bride was their aunt Anna Målsnes and the bridegroom was Andreas Kvale, of Sogndal, who was teaching school at Wangsnes in Sogn.

Kjellaug Ese told the story of the wedding gown: "My grandfather Lasse Målsnes bought it for his eldest son John's bride-to-be, but John was stricken with a fatal attack of appendicitis. Before his death, he asked his brother Arne to care for his fiancée. Arne fell in love with her and married her, so the girl for whom the costume was purchased did finally wear it."

It is her daughter who wears it in the painting, and the costume is still on the family farm. It is owned by Kjellaug Ese. She described the bodice or *bringetekkje* as a beautiful red with many silver brooches. The bridal crown and belt also contain spangles of silver.

The Ese sisters knew of the Dahl painting but had not seen it before. It was loaned to Vesterheim by Margaret Eckhardt of Prescott, Arizona. Her grandfather, E. H. Hobe, consul for Norway in Minnesota, is believed to have purchased the painting in Paris in 1902.

• • • •

Wedding customs varied slightly from district to district, but certain characteristics seem to have been rather general. The celebration was long. Three days were taken up by rather standard ceremony. The first day was the wedding itself. That included the trip to the church, either on horseback or by boat.

Two people other than the minister played important roles. One was the fiddler who led the ceremony and later accompanied the dancing. The other was the master of ceremonies who called all the shots at the feast. He was responsible for seeing that all the proper ritual was carried out. Some of this was of a humorous nature, but took a fixed form. Members of the party would say certain things, and others would respond with the expected phrases.

Gifts do not appear to have played a major role, but there were ceremonies in which the guests would put money in dishes that were passed around. The feast seems to have been a time at which the young couple got financial support to get established. The ceremonies relating to gifts of money were largely on the second day of the wedding.

The third day was one of eating and general festivity. This is when the bridal porridge was eaten. It consisted of a meal at which the rich sour cream pudding *rømmegrøt* was the main dish. It was theoretically prepared by the bride herself, and the master of ceremonies would give a humorous speech about the trials and tribulations that went into the making of the porridge. It was at this meal that the celebrated wedding spoons were used. According to tradition, the bride and the groom both ate from these linked utensils as a symbol of the unity between them. This practice may not be very old, but it seems to have been well-established by the 19th century because of the number of examples which exist from that time.

65

The third day also included much dancing and merry-making. It was a custom in Gudbrandsdalen to pull a large log into the yard to the sound of gunshots, something that also marked other high points in the wedding celebration. The bride and groom would go up on the log and drink to each other. When the bride and groom got down from the log, the other guests would go through the same ritual, drinking to each other. It all ended with dancing. This was terminated by another blast of guns and the master of ceremonies, assisted by the young people, would roll the log into the nearest stream.

Preceding the wedding ceremony at the church, a crown was worn by the bride. This was generally removed for the later part of the celebration so that the bride could dance with greater ease. After the removal of the crown, however, she put on a headdress that covered her hair. Exposed hair was associated with the virgin state and with luring an ultimate partner.

There is much else that could be said about Norwegian weddings, such as the custom in Voss of the bride bringing her baptismal blanket to the church and sitting on it during the wedding ceremony.

The above is drawn from a letter written by Marion Nelson, Director, Vesterheim, Decorah, Iowa, in response to an inquiry. He credits most of the information to Kristofer Visted and Hilmar Stigum, Vår Gamle Bondekultur (Our Old Peasant Culture): Oslo—J. W. Cappelins Forlag, 1911.

Wedding Spoons

Wedding spoons from Norway are in the Vesterheim collection. They have been popular since the late 18th century at the wedding dinner of the bride, in which rømmegrøt is the main dish. The bride ate from one spoon and the bridegroom from the other, symbolic of their union.

Fish in Norway

By Sigrid Marstrander

Since Norway is surrounded by water from North to South, and has so many rivers, fjords and lakes, it is natural that fish is an important part of the menu. When I lived in Norway, it was customary to have four days of fish, and three days of meat during the week. One large codfish would make several dinners for the average family, notably fish-balls and fish-pudding.

The man of the house usually did the fish-shopping. In the larger cities there were markets with cement water-tanks in which live fish were kept. The man went around inspecting them, and finally pointed to the one he wanted. The merchant hooked it up, and would sometimes kill it for the customer. *Torsk* (cod) was usually carried home to the kitchen alive. Of course, this was in the cities only. I remember once we had a new maid from far out in the country. When it came time to serve the dinner, she was found sitting in the stairway crying. She was afraid of the fish and couldn't kill it!

When Henning and I moved to America, I had a hard time finding the fresh-caught fish he liked so well. As he came in from work he would say, "I see we're having fish. I smelled it three blocks down the street."

Christmas in Norway

By Sigrid Marstrander
as told to Erna Oleson Xan

The crowning holiday of the year was Christmas. A month ahead, *Tante* Ida, with whom I lived, started housecleaning. Although there were no coal mines or factories in Trondheim to pollute the air, Anna P., the maid, and other workers cleaned the house from cellar to attic. Walls, ceilings, windows, curtains, cupboards—everything had to be shining for the Great Day. Poor Uncle Evenson was met by stepladders, brooms and buckets every time he came home, and complained that he felt uprooted and unwanted. Men often went to their clubs to escape the confusion.

After the cleaning was over, the baking started. Cookies enough to last through Easter were made at this season, for they were all so rich that they improved by ripening. For these cookies, fine Hungarian flour was used, and day by day hundreds of cookies were stored in tin boxes. This was one activity in which all women of the house took part, and even *Tante* Ida came out to the kitchen to help.

I beat the twelve eggs for *fattigmann* (poor man's cookies, a joke), and mixed in the flour and sugar. They were rolled out and cut leaf-thin with a *trinse*, a roller with a wavy edge, in diamond shape. Then I slit a hole in the middle of each one and turned one of the points through the slit. Anna P. had to fry them in lard, however, for it was dangerous for a young girl who might get splattered with the hot fat.

There were *Berlinerkranser* (Berlin wreaths), *smørkranser* (butter rings), *sandkaker* (sand cakes), following each other in fragrant succession.

One old lady apologized that she had only eighteen kinds of cookies for Christmas.

When this job was out of the way, Anna P. had to turn her hand to the special meats that were prepared each year. Christmas would not be complete without *sylte*. For this, a whole pig's head was boiled until tender. Then the bones, eyes and teeth were removed, leaving only the skin and meat. Now Anna P. mixed well-seasoned veal and white pork and stuffed it inside the head-skin, sewed it up tightly in a cloth and boiled it again until the veal and pork were tender. She then put it in a pan with a plate and big stone on top until it was compressed to three or four inches thick. Finally it was laid in a crock in a brine made of salt, sugar, vinegar and water.

There was no keeping me out of the kitchen while these Christmas preparations were going on. It was my delight to turn the handle of the meatgrinder for Anna P. when she made *fiskeboller* (fish balls) and fish pudding. *Fiskeboller* began as fresh haddock scraped from the bone and skin, and then put through the grinder twelve times. It took Anna P. almost a whole day to make enough *fiskeboller* to last over the holidays, for she had to stand there and keep adding cold boiled milk and cream to the paste, spoon by spoon, stirring all the while and sprinkling in salt and nutmeg. If she wanted to make fish pudding out of it, she added an egg, and placed it in a greased pan, then put it in a pan of hot water and steamed it in the oven until set. Fish pudding was served hot with a white sauce during the fish course at dinner, or with melted butter and capers, or with curry, shrimp or lobster sauce.

On Christmas Eve Day, fresh bread was made from white flour, butter, sugar, egg, yeast and lots of currants, raisins and citron. This was a great treat, for during the year rye bread was eaten, and the whole-grain flatbread made out in the country in large round sheets.

None of this good food could be touched until Christmas Eve which was the highlight of the entire holiday. I could hardly wait for Uncle and Aunt to get ready for church, for I myself had been dressed the entire afternoon, waiting like a fire-horse for the moment to jump into my outer wraps.

Darkness came at four o'clock. At five o'clock the church bells began to chime and kept it up for an hour, while everybody who could go to church streamed out of their houses in answer to the glad call. It was against the law to keep stores open after six o'clock, so even the clerks hurried out to attend the services.

As we walked along the many streets, candles flickered in the windows, and people's eyes twinkled in response. Soft snow was falling, and the great stained-glass windows were lighted from within, shining through the slanting flakes. The deep tones of the bells resounded in my ears as we entered into the great arched doors of the spicy-smelling, candle-lit cathedral. The people sat in carved wooden seats.

Now the bells stopped ringing and the minister came out in his finest ceremonial robe. It was white and full, gathered at the neck, with wide sleeves and skirt. This was worn over his black robe, and the little black-and white ruff showed about his neck. Over his white garment was a red velvet front piece with a golden cross embroidered on it. The congregation stood as he read the Christmas story from the Bible, and sat while he preached the sermon.

Singing took up much of the service: *Jeg Synger Julekvad* (I Sing a Hymn to Christmas), *Et Barn er Født i Bethlehem* (A Child is Born in Bethlehem), and the *Kimer, I Klokker* (Chime, Ye Bells):

"Chime, bells, chime
Now is the evening time
Now the stars up in the skies
Twinkle like the angels' eyes."

After the service, the grown-up Evenson children and their children joined us for Christmas dinner.

Oh, what a sight the wonderful Christmas feast presented when the family got home! The dining table had been laid with the finest white damask cloth. Candles burning in silver candelabra were reflected by sparkling crystal and silver. There were holly and spruce twigs in the center of the table, surrounding a mirror-pond covered with boric acid crystals, and edged with cotton "snow." On this pond the *Julenisser* (Christmas brownies) were playing.

Everybody loved everybody at Christmas, and everybody had to have a good time. Anna P. always dined with the family that night. The children helped her wait table. She felt it a great treat to eat with the family at Christmastime, though it was plain to be seen it was more of a social than a gastronomic pleasure. But Anna P. was up to the occasion. She put on her best manners, took small bites, little fingers forever up-curved. But everyone knew that when the meal was over, Anna P. would plump herself down at the kitchen table and eat so much that she could hardly move.

The first course was always fish pudding, the second was reindeer with cream gravy. Reindeer tasted like venison, but with a wilder flavor. Sometimes there was half a ptarmigan for each person instead. It also had a wild taste. This course was served with boiled potatoes, peeled, cooked and dried until mealy. There were always imported vegetables—Brussels sprouts, or *Petit Pois* from France, and native cabbage and carrots. It would not be complete without the country *flatbrød*.

For dessert a light pudding, perhaps made of rice with chopped almonds, sugar, gelatine, and topped with whipped cream. It was called rice cream, and was often served with a red fruit sauce, such as strawberry juice thickened with cornstarch.

When the meal was over, the children could think of nothing but the tree in the closed parlor. Everybody carried dishes to the kitchen. Anna P. had only to wash a plate or cup, and a half-dozen hands reached out to dry it. But the end of the meal was not yet, for the after-dinner coffee was not yet served, and to omit it would be unthinkable.

After that, *Tante* Ida and Uncle Evenson got up, and with great deliberation that made the children "crazy," went into the parlor and shut the doors behind them. This was so that no one would see them lighting the dozens of twisted red candles on the tree.

When they flung open the doors, there in the middle of the room was the tall green Norwegian spruce reaching to the ceiling with candles ablaze, and little Norwegian flags gleaming in the candlelight. With pride I looked at the little heart-shaped baskets I had made and filled with nuts and raisins. Real little Norwegian apples swung and twisted on the branches. Colored paper chains were looped about the tree. On the top was a big star, and little angels were on the branches.

Before the presents under the tree could be distributed, Uncle Evenson got down the Bible and read the Christmas story again. Then the family joined hands and circled the tree again and again, singing. The last song was always:

"You green and glittering tree, Good Day!
How welcome you are to us today
With your Norwegian flags, and candles alight
And high in the top the star so bright,
Yes, the star must shine thus
For it must remind us
Of the Savior Child that is born tonight."

The children could be held no longer. "Enough, Grandfather! Let us have the *tree!*"

I was too big to be appointed 'gift-bearer'. That had become the duty of the smallest cousins. Oh, how swiftly their little feet went, carrying gifts to the seated family. My lap was soon full—a fur ascot and muff, new mittens and a new dress. Christmas gifts were not something one bought at a shop, except for books. But the gifts were lovingly made at home in the secrecy of one's room. "Knock before you enter," was the pre-Christmas warning.

I remember the year that I had made for Uncle Evenson a "watch pillow," a little padded cushion for a man's watch to hang in at night. *Tante* Ida received from me an embroidered pillow-top, an elk with antlers done in brown and tan on dark red flannel. Delighted at my growing skill with the needle, she put her arms around my neck and kissed me.

The family burst into song all during the evening. Nuts were cracked. Apples and dried fruit were munched. Presently Uncle Evenson said his watch was tired and wanted to go to bed in its new little pillow. So we all trooped to bed, because all had to be up and dressed and at the Cathedral by seven the next morning. There were two other services on that beautiful, white Christmas day of my youth.

Nidaros Cathederal.

70

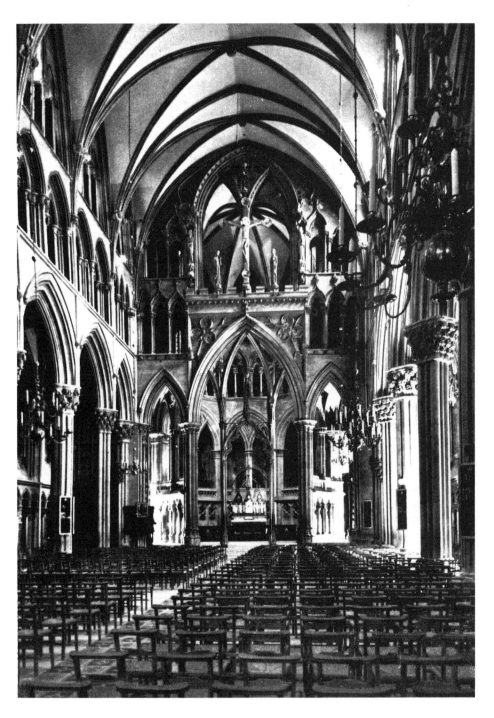

Interior of the Nidaros Cathederal, Trondheim, Norway. This is the church where Sigrid Marstrander was christened in 1891, confirmed in 1906 and married in 1919.

Tone: The Girl from Norway

By Henrietta Oleson Bear

On a sparkling morning in May, 1858, Tone (pronounced Tone-eh) Dalan stood at the rail of an ocean-going sailboat in the harbor of Christiania (Oslo, Norway). Her right hand closed firmly over the handle of a leather satchel in which she carried the immediate necessities for a six-week journey at sea. Below her the waters of the harbor danced and glittered in the sun but there was a chill in the air that the long snows of winter were reluctant to dispel.

Deep in the hold, sailors were flinging her heavy sea chest around, making room for it among many others that were loaded through the black hatch in a never-ending stream.

These chests, constructed of hard, smooth lumber from the mountain slopes of Norway, were made for rough handling. Reinforced with iron bands running over the arched lids and down the sides, they were painted blue or green and decorated with rosemaling in rich tones. The design embraced keyhole plates and locks and twined along the iron bands as if to direct the eye to its splendor and away from the massive contours of the chest itself. The artist included the initials of the emigrant as well as the year of departure from Norway. Almost every Norwegian-American home in the New World had one, and they must still be in existence today, since it is inconceivable that they would ever wear out.

The ponderous keys, hinged in the middle, folded like a jackknife, and 18-year-old Tone checked her satchel over and over to assure herself that the key was still there. Everything she owned in the world was in that chest—soft, wool-filled quilts, feather tick, a takedown spinning wheel, her Bible, and prayer books. Some of her clothes were of homespun or handwoven linen, and had to be guarded against moisture and moths. Carefully wrapped parcels of *Gammel Ost* and *Prim Ost* had been tearfully tucked in by mother, and father had slipped in his own hymnal at the last moment.

"Ja Far! Far!" (Oh, Father, Father) Tone sobbed, her blue eyes straining down to the water where an old man sat in a rowboat waiting for the ship to glide silently out of the harbor. His white head was thrown back as his own eyes searched the rail for a last glimpse of his daughter. A breeze lifted the silver hair from his forehead and the young girl's heart throbbed with pain at the thought of never seeing that dear head again. How often she had stood behind her father's chair, combing and brushing his hair while he dozed. She loved to feel the silky strands cling to her fingers and fall into a soft roll over his collar. Mother would scold and tell her to let her father nap in peace, but he demurred. This helped him to rest all the more comfortably, he said.

A wild impulse shook Tone from head to foot. She couldn't go! She must find the sailors and beg them to hoist her chest from the hold again and fly with it down the ladder and into her father's boat before it was too late!

But the impulse died. She knew she couldn't turn back. Brother Jon was waiting for her in America. He had gone two years earlier and his wondrous letters had filled her heart with promise. . .America the rich. America the free. America the land of opportunity such as no one in Norway had ever dreamed of. Sitting around the table in their little home near the fjord, Tone and the family had read and reread the letters.

"Think, Father," Jon wrote. "A great farm just for the asking! Cousin Bjorn is on such a farm right now. Eighty acres of black, rolling soil in mid-east Wisconsin. He has been clearing his land, and already has a snug log house built from his own trees. Next spring he will sow a small grain field, and then will come a barn and some cows. He will be king over here. We all will. Someday soon I'll have a farm, too. You must let Tone come. There is work for everyone here. The land jingles with silver dollars. She'll marry a rich farmer and be mistress of a fine home in the country. . ."

On the next page he would appeal to the mother. "What would you think, Mother, if Tone could turn her cows out to pasture in plain sight of her house! Everyone has pasture here. Plenty. The cattle are so fat they can hardly get through the barn doors at night. The rich grass grows everywhere and in all the world there wouldn't be enough cows to eat it all. Haying? If you could see the haystacks here! No grubbing along streams or fence lines to find a few wisps of hay to stuff in the barn for the dark months ahead. . .There is a boat sailing from Christiania in May. Let Tone come. We'll be rich in a few years and send for the rest of you."

Tone stayed at the rail. Her heart was breaking but the determination to become part of Jon's new world was too strong. She stood there long after the little boat with her beloved father had faded into the mist of the harbor.

The six-week journey was beset by storms and hardships. Food became stale and moldy. Children were sick and underfoot. Tone was terrified at the great waves breaking over the ship. Little children had to be watched for fear they would be washed overboard, and older men, accustomed to the placid fjords of their homeland, had no legs to cope with the pitching decks of the ship.

During one of the worst storms a young woman, in the last months of pregnancy, (her child was not scheduled to be born until they reached the new land) began feeling labor pains, brought on prematurely from fright and the reeling turbulence of the vessel. The Norwegian women aboard sprang to her side, Tone among them. They tried frantically to convince her that this would pass if she remained calm and as quiet as possible. But despite their efforts the pains persisted. Hour after hour the tormented soul writhed in her bed and cried for help. The women cried with her, smoothing the damp hair from her forehead and praying. To no avail. Early in the darkness of the stormy daybreak, a tiny little girl was born and the exhausted mother was dead a few hours later.

The wails of the premature infant were so feeble no one expected her to live. What a disaster! The women moaned and wept. Their hearts went out to those who would receive this terrible news when the ship landed. If they could keep the baby alive, at least that would in some way console the relatives. Tone wrapped the whimpering foundling in a sheepskin and swaddled it further with the warmest blankets she could find. She pressed the bundle to her breast and rocked back and forth.

Eventually the mother of a 6-month-old baby heard of the tragedy and came from her quarters to investigate. Her compassion was so aroused by the plight of the orphan that she offered to nourish and care for it along with her own child until they reached land and found the relatives. When the time came, however, there was no one who expected a young pregnant woman, not to mention a newborn infant, so the woman who had kept this little waif alive adopted her.

By coincidence the woman was among the group boarding the train for the long trek to Wisconsin, settling in much the same area as Tone. In consequence the child who had literally been thrust into the world on the storm-tossed waves of the Atlantic became a friend of Tone's for life. (I met her just once, kneeling in prayer at my grandmother Tone's deathbed, sorrowfully parting with her old friend.)

Tone melded into American ways in no time at all. The language barrier was extremely difficult at first but she was quick and intelligent and got along somehow. After a short time with Jon she secured the position of 'hired girl' with an Englishwoman named Mrs. Johnson. The first days went smoothly enough for the anxious young emigrant. Her talented manner with children stood her in good stead and she knew well how to peel and cook potatoes and onions.She caught on fast to the strange English style of making beds and tried hard to please her employer in every way.

But one day Mrs. Johnson gave Tone a basin and told her to go to the cellar and bring up carrots for dinner. Tone took the basin and started down the stairs. What was that English word c-a-r-r-o-t-s? She had forgotten and panicked on the bottom step. Tears of shame filled her eyes (she often told me this story) and she longed for her old home in Norway. She did not know what to put in the basin and stood helpless until Mrs. Johnson came to her rescue, comforting and consoling her. This episode cemented an already mutual affection.

Tone had Sunday afternoons to herself. As soon as the Sunday dinner work was completed, she set off across the marsh to visit her brother Jon. The path was often wet and in many places it was necessary to walk a narrow plank laid over the mud. On one of these Sundays, the summer wind blowing her brown hair around her face, Tone, carefully maneuvering on the plank but full of the joy of life, looked up into the ocean-blue eyes of a tall and handsome young man. Neither one could immediately proceed, and Tone's cheeks turned red in consternation. She had never met anyone on the marsh before and was taken off guard when the young man chided her a little in Norwegian. Where was she going, and who of the two would have to back up to dry ground?

The result was an instant love affair and although they did not meet often, both knew that destiny had a hand in their lives. Love can find a way and now and then Tone and Hans found themselves together.

Jon approved of this alliance. Hans came from a good family. Their large farm was worked on shares with their sons. All the married brothers had quarters in the big house for their families. Hans, although a little on the wild side, was steady enough, and his heart belonged to blue-eyed Tone.

Following their marriage, Hans and Tone moved into a corner of the parental homestead. Both Hans and Tone were hard-working and thrifty. John (my father), Mary, and Julia were born in orderly succession. Tone helped Hans to make ends meet. Hans helped her in writing letters home to Norway. Her education had been confined to her catechism days, which was more or less sufficient, but letter writing was not a strong point. Hans followed her dictation for the messages that went over the sea concerning her beloved husband and their three beautiful children.

Several heavenly years went by. Tone's life was completely centered around her home. She made cheese, butter, and bread for her robust young husband and growing children. They had a few chickens and a cow of their own. The chickens were well-fed, and their eggs filled baskets to overflowing. At the store Tone exchanged eggs for sugar and flour. Cream from the rich milk was sold to buy material for Hans' stout work clothes and shoes for the children. By "picking a penny here and picking a penny there," she told me, they were headed for a life in paradise as compared to what they had known in Norway.Tone couldn't believe this life of happiness and plenty.

The idyll was not to last. Ominous news began rolling up from the South. Tone's beautiful new country was splitting across the middle over the question of slavery. Tone had never seen a black person, let alone a slave, but she instinctively knew this was a grave situation. Before she completely realized what was happening, young men and husbands were in blue uniforms, Hans among them, and life was never the same again.

Tone did not see Hans again until the day she looked up from working in the garden to see her emaciated young husband staggering up the road, half-dead with dysentery, brought on, he told her, from eating a piece of poisoned peach pie in Tennessee where he had been fighting. Whatever the cause, he died in a few weeks and Tone was left to join the growing ranks of young women in widow's weeds at the Winchester Church.

Tone always said this period was the most difficult in her life. She continued to have a home with Hans' folks until some years after the war, when she met and married Joseph Omness. Joseph was an industrious, steadfast man several years her junior. Tone was a fine looking woman who appeared to be several years younger than her age, while Joseph looked considerably older than his, so they made a good-looking, suitably matched couple. Their marriage lasted 64 years—until Tone died in 1932 at the age of ninety-three. Joseph followed her to the cemetery less than a year later.

The Norwegians changed their names when they came to this country, usually adding 'son' to the given name of the emigrant's father. Thus Hans, who was the son of Ole in Norway, took the name of Hans Oleson. When my grandmother Tone married a second time she took the name of Omness, but when they retired to Winneconne in later years they went by the name of Olson, spelled without the "e".

Joseph Omness was the only paternal grandfather I ever knew, and no amount of tales about the dear, dead Hans were of interest to me in my childhood. I loved Grandpa Joe. He was the patient fixer of broken toys and the Rock of Gibraltar of my childhood. I often heard Grandma say, not in his presence of course, that Joe, while the salt of the earth, was no match for Hans' quick, energetic ways. But Joseph was an exemplary father to her three children and even during the wild-oats-sowing days of my handsome father (he resembled Hans, Grandma said) there was never a cross word between them. And despite the fact that I was named Henrietta (Hans had Anglicized his name to Henry when he went to war) the ties between us were strong and binding. There was no malice in this precious old gentleman who was loved by us all.

On one of my childhood visits to this home, the china arm and hand of my cloth-bodied doll became disengaged and crashed to the floor, breaking in many pieces. My heart was shattered along with fragments at my feet, and of course the tears flowed.

Grandpa Joe witnessed this drama and in time his brows began to knit. He never moved or spoke in haste, but when we saw his brow lift in deep horizontal lines we could be sure something was about to happen. I stood by his side as he studied the doll, turning it this way and that, stemming the flow of sawdust from the arm socket, brows knitting even more intensely than before. Finally he rose deliberately from his chair and went out to the shed. When he came back he carried a small block of blond wood and sat down again.

Still sniffling over my misfortune, I had no idea what he was up to when he took out his jackknife and began whittling on the wood. He measured the sound arm of my doll and whittled some more! Could Grandpa make a new arm? He could and he did. When his cutting and filing and sanding and measuring was finished, he held in his hand a remarkable facsimile of the broken member. Each little finger curved delicately like that of its counterpart. Slowly and with great pains he fastened it into the empty socket, and I had a sound doll once more.

In her second marriage Tone ruled the home, and this was agreeable to Joseph. He greatly admired and respected her. She was thrifty, could work circles around him, might even see a solution to a problem several days before he did, but it was Joseph who, like the example of the tortoise and the hare, brought the matter to a successful conclusion. They produced one child together, a little girl named Hannah. As could be expected in this orderly household, the sibling relationship between Hannah and the three older children was normal and affectionate.

Until Grandma died she and Joseph spent their last years in the home of my parents during the winters. But Joseph lived the last ten months of his life in far-off Minnesota with Hannah. I never saw him again, but I have never forgotten him.

My childhood was saddened by the thought of my dear Grandma Tone leaving her father and mother in Norway to brave the stormy Atlantic, knowing she might never go back. I loved my long vacations with her, but I always knew that further down the river connecting my home in Oshkosh with Winneconne, my father and mother awaited my return. Leaving home as Grandma Tone did was quite common in those days. Those who left Norway must have been sustained by the hope that they would return some day. In many instances, though, they did not. Grandma's farewells from Norway, like so many of her contemporaries, were final and irreversible. My fainting heart could never have accepted that.

Henrietta O. Bear is the sister of Erna Oleson Xan, author of this book. Mrs. Bear was married forty years to the late Fred Bear, noted archer and big game hunter. Mr. Bear was the founder and chairman of Bear Archery Company of Gainesville, Florida, home of the Fred Bear Museum and its wildlife displays.

Grandma Was Frugal

By Henrietta Oleson Bear

In the early 1900s I spent most of my school vacations with my grandparents in Winneconne, Wisconsin. Coming from a family of seven children, I loved these vacations. I received my grandparents' total affection whereas at home I had to share the love and attention of our parents with all my sisters and brothers. On the other hand, at home we enjoyed delicious meals, while at Grandma's the food, though wholesome, was often very plain.

In this scrupulous Norwegian household there were two sets of dishes. One was of heavy ironstone, plain white, and so heavy I could hardly lift the plates. These were for everyday use. The other set was daintier with an all-over pattern of brown leaves and azalea-like flowers. These dishes were kept in the yellow pine corner cupboard in the best sitting room and were used only when we had company. This was quite often, however, because so many of our relatives and friends came regularly from the village of Winchester to shop. They brought baskets of eggs and cream from their farms and sat down to Grandma's noon dinners.

There were no telephones, but Grandma was always ready for these unannounced visits. There never seemed to be any flurry. The dinner, considerably embellished from the plain fare when we were alone, was on the table in no time, and all heads were bowed while Grandpa said grace in Norwegian.

In hindsight, perhaps I do know why Grandma was up to this situation. First, she knew her visitors and their shopping routines. After the noon meal they had to complete their shopping and get back home in time for chores. Second, the menu varied but little. We either had fried pork and milk gravy with boiled potatoes and carrots, or fried fish and fried potatoes with pickled beets. These menus were bolstered by homemade bread with butter and jelly. For dessert we had some of the white cake Grandma baked every Saturday. And coffee, of course.

The big dining-sitting room was heated by an iron cookstove. On all but the hottest days of summer, it was used to cook the food, boil the coffee, and heat the water. In hot weather coffee was brewed fresh on the kerosene stove in the summer kitchen. Coffee was one of life's staples and no one came through our door without being offered a cup together with a large sour-cream cookie.

Grandma thought it was her duty to teach me to bake. I learned almost nothing, because I wanted so desperately to be out playing instead. (In most of the homes on Water Street there was a hired girl to do the baking.) Also, since my heart wasn't in it, my attention span was short and Grandma's patience was even shorter. She would take the spoon from my hand and stir the batter herself. She would try me next on sifting flour, but there, too, I failed. The flour spilled into the cupboard, which she told me was a sinful waste. I learned to scoop up every trace of it and pour it back into the bowl.

In any event there was no escaping until the baking was done. The ritual never varied. We made a white cake first, with jelly between the layers and a soggy meringue frosting on top. Then came the unfrosted, everyday molasses cake, and last the sour-cream cookies. It all took until near noon, and by the time Grandma untied one of her long, gray aprons from around my neck, my friends, tired of waiting, were scattered all up and down the block.

We did the baking in the large pantry just off the dining-sitting room. All the cooking utensils were in cupboards there, as well as a pump with a galvanized sink and drain. There was also a small table beside which, every afternoon at 4 o'clock, Grandma sat down for a cup of coffee and a sour-cream cookie. If any of my friends were on hand and Grandma wasn't too busy, she made 'coffee' for us, too—one of the tasty sour-cream cookies, and tiny little jelly sandwiches that fit on the precious three-inch butter pats that were part of her good china—a delight unsurpassed in our young lives. Now, many years later, two of those doll-sized saucers hang on a cypress wall in my Florida kitchen along with a collection of a hundred others inspired by the types I have treasured from my childhood.

The car that Grandpa drove into—and through—the garage.

Facing the street at the back of our lot was a small building that served now as a garage for Grandpa's car, one of the first model T Fords in Winneconne. One day, returning from a trial run with this machine, Grandpa became confused between brake and gas lever and the car plunged through the end of the garage, boards cracking in every direction. Grandma, who had been looking from the window, flew out the door with me close behind to witness a rare upbraiding directed at her husband. Acquisition of this car was one of the few things they had seriously disagreed about, and Grandma was full of righteous indignation. She eventually rode in this machine, but mostly her journeys were spent in prayer. Grandpa's accident left an imprint on me, too. To this day I am nervous about driving a car into a garage.

On the large back lot Grandpa operated a veritable truck garden. To the left of the path were neat rows of vegetables—potatoes, onions, and carrots. There were no tomatoes, for he firmly believed that tomatoes were "poison." On the right of the path he planted berry bushes—raspberries, currants, and gooseberries, as well as a healthy strawberry bed. In addition, there was a lovely grape arbor near the house where the vines hung heavy with grapes.

Nothing was ever wasted in this household. Potatoes, carrots, and cabbages were stored in the little black cellar under the pantry. Along improvised shelves in a back room Grandpa arranged onions to dry for the winter. We seldom ate berries fresh from the bushes, since cream was saved for butter and cooking. Cream soured in thunderstorms, but was put to good use in the cookies. The berries, cooked in a very light syrup, were put up in quart jars and stored in a separate pantry where the temperature was just right for keeping food without refrigeration. These glass jars of "sauce" accompanied every "company meal" throughout the year.

Grapes were not stored. We often had a bowlful in the middle of the oilcloth-covered table. But grapes spoiled rapidly and drew flies, so this was discouraged. I found it delightful to go to the arbor and pick a bunch of amethyst grapes to eat on the spot. As with everything Grandpa cultivated, they grew in profusion. To prevent waste, Grandma cooked some of them into juice, which was brought from the cellar for callers.

Sometimes Aunt Julia came home from Ironwood, Michigan, for a visit. These visits were not the happiest times for her parents. Aunt Julia crimped her hair with a curling iron heated in the chimney of the dresser lamp. She ran up dressmaking bills, and spent far more for groceries than was customary in this household. She scoffed at her mother's Spartan ways and took over much of the baking. No more watery egg-white frostings now. Julia knew how to boil sugar and milk and make fancy fillings between the layers, instead of Grandma's jelly. She skimmed sweet cream from the milk and poured it over rich puddings. She used real butter in the cookies. When friends or relatives from Winchester brought gifts of pork or beef that Grandma could stretch for several meals, Julia cooked it all at once. We lived high during her visits.

Julia arrived with a barrel of empty glass jars and returned with jars filled with cooked fruits and berries. Grandpa paid the freight. Grandma furnished the sugar, not outwardly complaining, but full of wonder at the extravagance of her daughter. After Julia left for home, Grandpa and I missed the rich cakes and sweet cream for a while, but it would have been unthinkable to mention it.

One of Grandma's treats was to make Norwegian *grøt* for us. A tasty, porridge-like dish, it is made from rice and skim milk. The hot *grøt* was poured onto a flat plate and sprinkled with cinnamon and sugar. In the center we made a well for a generous pat of butter which melted and ran in delicious rivulets through the cinnamon and sugar. At each plate was a small bowl of milk, and the style for *grøt*-eaters was to fill one's spoon with porridge and dip it into the cool milk before eating. It never tasted the same if the milk was poured directly over the *grøt!* On a visit to Norway in 1964 a lovable cousin whom I had never met was enchanted to see that we knew how to eat this famous Norwegian dish in the true ethnic fashion. I have, in turn, taught my daughter and foster son and their children, and their children, to eat *grøt* in proper style.

In Grandma's category of sins nothing surpassed that of wasting food unless it was breaking the Sabbath. One of the most serious ways of breaking the Sabbath, she maintained, was the use of scissors on Sunday.

"Every scrap of material or paper that you cut on Sunday will be burned on the back of your hand when you die," she told me. Inability to cut paper dolls made rainy Sundays interminable. Another thing that stabbed like a knife was being denied the Sunday comics which Grandma was sure were the works of the devil. On these occasions I missed my home in Oshkosh, Wisconsin, where, after Sunday School, almost any pleasure was allowed.

Those years of Grandma's cooking were responsible, I suppose, for my unfaltering acceptance of food to this day. I can eat anything, cooked any way, at any time.

Thurine Olson Oleson and her husband John H. Oleson, parents of Erna Oleson Xan, were married 50 years on May 26, 1936. They lived on a farm at *Waupaca, Wisconsin.* Wisconsin My Home *is the story of Thurine Oleson as told to her daughter.* From the collection of Erna Oleson Xan.

How I Wrote 'Wisconsin My Home'

By Erna Oleson Xan

We owe it all to a little foreign nun.

In late January, 1941, when I was living in Birmingham, Alabama, I received a telephone call from my sister Henrietta in Oshkosh, Wisconsin. She told me the sad news that our father, John H. Oleson, had had a severe stroke and was not expected to live. They had taken him to the Catholic hospital nearby. She said that all the children had come home and were helping, but that Mama would not leave him day or night. "Only I know what he wants," she would say.

Immediately I packed my bags and left by train. At the hospital, Mama lay on a cot alongside Papa's bed, and my chair was at the head of the aisle in between. I could wait on them both. We were fed by baskets of delectable food which Henrietta sent over.

After about two weeks of this, a little foreign nun beckoned me into the hall. "You know we cannot save your Papa," she said. "But if you do not get your Mama's mind off him, you are going to bury them in the same grave."

This frightened me, and we girls discussed what on earth we could do. Then it came to me—her happy childhood on a farm at Winchester, Wisconsin, where her parents lived when they had come from Norway, and where she was born.

"Mama," I whispered, "do you remember any of your mother's recipes? How she made bread and sausage and things?"

It was as if a light had been turned on in Mama's face. "Oh, yes," she whispered back. "I've used them all my life."

The first recipe we got down was *Bestemor's* (Grandma's) bread, eaten as it came out of the oven, slathered with fresh butter and plum preserves. We wrote how to make cheese, and cookies, pickled pigs' feet; thick, rich soups, and puddings. It took days to tell each story in low voices or whispers. Sometimes dear Papa would wake up and ask what we were doing, and he'd sort of smile.

The next subject was *Bestefar's* (Grandpa's) friends. Grandpa could not speak English, and his Irishman neighbor friend could not speak Norwegian. But for the next 30 years they never lacked a child interpreter. The church sexton, the town treasurer, all were told about in this Friendship chapter.

Mama was beginning to look much better. When I saw the Sister in the hall, she would pat my back and say, "Goot!"

The third subject was the church which some of our relatives had founded on top of a high hill near the farm. Mama had much to say about that. Her memory was astounding. She had grown up in the church, and loved it. There had been a split one time, and her folks went one way and Papa's folks another.

One day in the hall, the old Sister asked what we were doing, and I told her. She was so pleased. "Dot is goot syology (psychology)!" she beamed.

In five weeks our dear Papa died, and Mama's two homes were sold. She went to Rice Lake, Wisconsin, to live with sister Stella and Ole Thompson. Our sister Clara lived nearby.

Mama was tenderly taken care of, but broken-hearted. Several years later she came to spend the winter with me in Alabama. She began to cry, not from abuse or neglect, but that she didn't have a home any more. What on earth was I going to do?

Ah! The childhood's story. Placing a small rocker near my typewriter, I got her to crocheting and talking. "Tell me about your courtship," I said. When we finished that, it was Early Marriage and Children. As they came out of the machine, I laid the papers in a pile beside me on the table.

One day I counted through them and said, "Mama, do you know we have 75,000 words here, enough for a book?"

This made her laugh out loud. "A book? Out of that simple stuff? Who in the world would read it?"

I replied, "Lots of people like this kind of reading. It reminds them of their own lives."

We finished up with Golden Wedding during the Depression. I retyped it all and sent it off.

The first two publishers sent it right back. (Maybe Mama was right. Too simple!)

Meanwhile, back home at the University of Wisconsin, the Press had hired a new, young editor, Thompson Webb. He said to his Board of Directors at the Press, "In 100 years of publishing history, we have put out only learned treatises. What we need is a social history of Wisconsin."

Just about that time, in came "Wisconsin My Home." I did not hear from them for about eight months, except that they had received the manuscript. One time I sent them a letter suggesting towns where our relatives lived and where the book might sell. They replied, "Don't worry, Mrs. Xan, your book is being read by all kinds of people—social workers, experts on the Norwegian scene, farmers, housewives. We will let you know what they say."

They made only one complaint. Where was the farm called "Laine" in Norway? All farms in Norway had a name from antiquity and were all listed on maps. But the scholars could not find this one. Now what? That's what Mama had told me, and her memory was as clear as a silver bell. Her parents, she said, had lived in their first home on the "Laine" farm. One day I found an old address book, and in the back, there it was. *Bestefar's* first farm in Norway was called *Leine* (pronounced "Lay-ne.") I had just misspelled it.

The book came out in December 1950. We have letters from all over the nation. It has been in print ever since, in one form or another.

Editor's Note: *Excerpts from* Wisconsin My Home *are reprinted in this book by kind permission of the publisher and copyright holder, The University of Wisconsin Press.* Wisconsin My Home *is as interesting as the story of its origin is touching.*

Above: Sauland church in Telemark, Norway. Erna's maternal grandmother, Thorhild Andreasdatter Bøe, was christened, confirmed and married here.

Left: Heddal stavkirke, Telemark, one of 30 stave churches left in Norway. Erna's maternal grandfather, Mathis Olson Hefre, was christened and confirmed here, and was married to Thorhild Bøe at the Sauland church about twenty miles away. Many of Erna's ancestors are buried in these two churchyards.

Photographs from the collection of Erna Oleson Xan.

Aurlandsfjord, Sogn, Norway. Photograph by Darrell Henning.

Valdres, Norway. Photograph by Darrell Henning.

Aurlandsfjord, Sogn, Norway. Photograph by Darrell Henning.

Telemark Fylkesmuseum, Skien, Norway. Photograph by Darrell Henning.

Christmas table-setting at Norsk Folkemuseum, Oslo, Norway. Photograph by Darrell Henning.

87

Norsk Folkemuseum, Oslo, Norway. Photograph by Darrell Henning.

Pre-19th-century home furnishings; at upper left is a trestle table top. Telemark Fylkesmuseum, Skien, Norway. Photograph by Darrell Henning.

Valdres, Norway. Photograph by Darrell Henning.

Private country home, Grimdalen, Telemark, Norway. Photograph by Darrell Henning.

Food Preparation in Norway

By Thurine Oleson
as told to Erna Oleson Xan
Reprinted from Wisconsin My Home

I heard plenty about the delicious food in Norway. One of their favorite dishes was clabbered milk with the cream left on it. Another was egg pancakes. I was always amused to hear them refer to egg yolks as "egg plums." They ate a lot more meat in Norway than in America—beef, mutton, and pork. In the spring it would be lamb and veal. Some salted meats would last the year 'round. Fish was always on hand—herring, trout, and *lutefisk*. Mother said she was good at catching speckled trout in the mountain streams. The men did fishing with nets. They often broiled their catch over the coals in the kitchen fireplace.

But the main dish was a pudding called *grøt* (pronounced "grout"). It was usually eaten for supper. A common variety was made with milk and flour, salted to taste and called *velling*. Another popular kind was *potetgrøt*. Mother made it this way: First she cooked potatoes until they were falling to pieces, them mashed them in the water they were cooked in. Into this she sifted flour and stirred until it was thick, seasoning it with the coarse cooking salt from the jar by the fireplace. The flour would lump a little, of course, and she would stir it vigorously with a *grøtturu* that Father had made for her. She was not satisfied until the *grøt* was white and smooth, and never liked to feel little uncooked lumps of dough in her mouth.

Now it was ready to dip up on plates, with a generous lump of butter in a hollow of the steaming pudding, whose sides would presently be trickling with yellow streams. Each place would be set with a plate of this, a spoon and a cup of milk. How happy the family was to sit down to the good meal, say the blessing, and go to eating. To eat *grøt*, one first dipped a spoonful of it into the melted butter, then into the cup of milk, then into the hungry waiting mouth it went. No one ever tired of it.

Risgryngrøt was made of rice, flour, milk, water, and salt cooked together until real soft, stirred all the time with the *grøtturu*. At table, sugar and cinnamon were sprinkled over this before dipping into the milk. They did not have this kind as often, because rice had to be bought in town.

If there was special company, or if it was Christmas or Easter, and surely whenever there was a new baby, then *rømmegrøt* was made out of pure cream (*rømme*). Mother thought nothing of using a quart of cream for this delicious dish. She poured it into a round bottom iron kettle and put it over the fire. When it began to boil, she began to sift in flour, and salt to taste, and stirred it until the cream rose to the top. It had to be stirred with the *grøtturu* every moment to keep from lumping and sticking to the bottom of the kettle.

Now, this *grøtturu* was made from a certain peeled and polished pine limb, with a ring of five up-shooting small branches at the end. Father had cut the branches to about three inches long before he peeled and polished it. The handle was about fifteen inches long. Big Helga or one of the older girls had to stand beside Mother, who was sifting the flour into the cream, and twirl the handle of this primitive egg beater between their palms, while the five prongs kept the *grøt* in swirls and waves every minute. When the *grøt* became thick, milk was added to the right amount, and if the cream had not risen properly, as much butter as needed was added to make it richer. This, too, was served hot on plates. It was often sprinkled with sugar and cinnamon before dipping into the melted butter and milk.

If Mother was going to give this as a gift, she would carry as much as a two-quart panful to the new mother. The top would be stuck full of sugar lumps or sprinkled with sugar and cinnamon. Then she would say, "I have brought you some *grøt* to make you strong." In winter, this pudding would keep until it was used up, and the new mother served some of it each day. She was supposed to drink a lot of homemade beer, too, to make milk. When my mother had babies in Norway, she had such excellent care and diet that by the time she got out of bed, there would be a dimple on top of every knuckle on her hands. The babies in Norway were so fat from rich mother's milk, and the mild *rømmegrøt* fed them later, that they were like balls of butter, and seldom sick. Babies did not have special beds in Norway, but were bundled up and put to sleep above the mother's head on the pillow.

There was a trained woman who went around in the fall to bake the winter's supply of *flatbrød* (flatbread). This was a sort of crisp, cracker-like bread baked in round sheets, which they ate daily, since yeast bread was used only for Christmas and Easter. First they took a quart of flour, a cup of cornmeal, and a cup of whole wheat flour, and sifted it with salt to taste. They then scalded it with boiling water and mixed it into a dough, adding four tablespoons of butter in the process. Now this mass was allowed to cool while Mother prepared the table for rolling out, for it needed lots of room. The long thin rolling pin she used for this purpose was carved by Father, and was grooved in spirals to spread the dough better. When the dough was cool enough to handle, she sprinkled flour on her mixing board on the table and began to work a ball of the dough into an even round shape as big as a milk pan, maybe seventeen inches across. In the meantime the *flatbrød* woman was busy scouring off the stove top or griddle on which these sheets were to be baked. She had to make it shine, for Mother wanted no little black burned specks through her bread. In America *flatbrød* was baked right on the lids of the wood cook stove.

The secret of making *flatbrød* was to roll the sheets so thin that they barely hung together. To lift this big thin sheet off the table and onto the stove and not break it, Mother used a long wooden spatula called a *brødskuru*. She started at one side of the sheet and rolled the *flatbrød* gently over the spatula, then unrolled it carefully onto the hot griddle. Just as much skill was needed to turn it when it was browned on one side. Mother slipped the spatula under it, and with her hand steadied it till it was flipped over on the other side to brown. When it was baked, it was lifted back onto the table to cool. After this, the sheets were stacked like round cardboards and stored in a cool, clean place. *Flatbrød* kept all winter and was eaten at will. It was always as crisp as a fresh soda cracker. To eat it, one broke off a small piece and buttered it. We often ate it unbuttered, broken up in a bowl of milk.

Another popular bread was *lefse*, but it could not be stored like *flatbrød*. It had a potato base. To make *lefse*, Mother took twenty boiled Irish potatoes, mashed them fine and added two tablespoons of melted butter or a half-cup of cream, and salt to taste. Then she added enough flour to permit rolling out. If it became too dry, she added a half cup of potato water. The ball of *lefse* dough that was pinched off would make the size of a dinner plate when rolled out. She used a smooth rolling pin for this. The dough had to be very thin and was baked on the griddle or top of the stove. When it was slightly brown, Mother turned it over with the *brødskuru* and baked it on the other side. *Lefse* was not crisp like *flatbrød*, but limp and soft like a pancake. It was folded over when taken off the stove. Norwegians liked *lefse* hot or cold, and buttered. Some rolled it up like a pancake and ate it out of hand. Pickled pigs' feet or *lutefisk* were a favorite accompaniment.

This *lutefisk* was a much prized dish in Norway. It was made from a fish called *torsk* (cod) caught in the ocean in summer. It was cleaned and cut in halves lengthwise and laid on stones to dry in the sun for about three or four weeks, until the halves became very hard. Boatloads of this dried fish were shipped to other countries. The housewife had to know a long time ahead when she wanted to serve *lutefisk*, because it had to be soaked in water for two weeks. Even then, *lutefisk* was not a dish one could make up her mind to prepare between dinner and supper, because now it had to be soaked again in lye water that was made from the ashes of peeled maple wood. It must stand in this lye water until the fish was soft enough to allow the fingers to touch through the meat when pinched.

Yet the meat was not ready to cook. It must be soaked again in clear water overnight. The next day it was skinned and cut into serving pieces. Then one must place it in a cloth and drop it into boiling salted water and boil it until the meat was firm, three to five minutes. *Lutefisk* went to the table on a platter, strewn with melted butter, or a rich milk gravy with a lot of butter in it. It was served with mashed potatoes and *lefse*.

Christmas was celebrated for three weeks in Norway. Therefore, a good deal of butchering and baking had to be done beforehand. Stacks of *flatbrød* had been put aside, and now it was time to make the cookies called *kringler* and *fattigmand*. *Kringler* were made in the shape of a ring. For this, Mother creamed together a cup of butter and a cup of sugar and added two eggs, beaten till very light. To this she added a half cup of milk and one teaspoon of caraway seed. Enough flour was added to make a dough stiffer than cake batter, but not as stiff as regular cookie dough. She then pinched off a small piece, rolled it under her hands to about six or eight inches long, deftly tied it into a bowknot, and baked it on a pan in a hot oven. These simply melted in one's mouth.

The name "*fattigmand*" (poor man) is a joke, for it is a very rich cookie. Cream was the fat in this, three tablespoons of it, mixed with three table- spoons of sugar. To this was added three eggs and the whole beaten for fifteen minutes with a wooden spoon until it was light yellow and fluffy. One teaspoon each of cardamom seed and of brandy were added. Now enough flour was sifted and folded in to make a stiff dough. A plain rolling pin was used to roll it very thin. It was cut in squares or oblongs with a knife, and each square pricked with a knife-point. When *fattigmand* was baked in hot grease in a skillet, the square corners all turned up. After they were slightly browned, they were lifted out of the skillet and laid on a board to cool. *Fattigmand* had to be stored in boxes in another room, out of temptation, to await the feasting time. Christmas was a great season for visiting and company, and Mother was always amply prepared. She taught all her daughters to make these good Norwegian dishes.

Summertime in Norway

By Thurine Oleson
as told to Erna Oleson Xan
Reprinted from Wisconsin My Home

In summer, when the men tended the crops, the women had to take the cattle and sheep to the *seter* (mountain pasture) where the grass was lush and green. It was just after St. Hans's Day (June 24) that they went up . . . Father owned his own *seter*. You had to climb a mountain to get there. Then there was a lovely green valley where the *seter* buildings were. Two girls had to watch the cows all day. Nearly every cow wore a bell, and all the ringing together made such a beautiful sound in the clear mountain air. . .

In our family, it was Mother who went to the *seter* with the herd. She loved to tend the cows and make butter and cheese. Besides, it was a delightful change from routine, like going to a wonderful mountain resort where the air was fresh and the sky vast and blue. She would take at least one of the older children to help look after the cattle, as well as one of the chore girls, and of course, the baby would have to be with her. Little brother John used to love to go because he got all the sweet cream he could eat up there. The home and the other children were left in the care of Father and Big Helga. Father would visit up on the mountain often, to get up wood and do anything else that he could, but Mother never left her post all summer . . . .

While mother was gone up to the *seter*, great activity was taking place at home . . . . The hay was cut and raked by hand, and that was slow work. Grain was cut by sickle. It was an older girl's job to cut and bind the straw into bundles. The main crops raised were barley, wheat, oats, and potatoes. The barley was ground into flour and used for mush, or for malt to make the *juleøl* (Christmas ale). The oats were fed to the stock, and some of the crop was used to make *flatbrød*. Some of the wheat was ground whole for baking, some made into white flour for the Christmas and Easter celebrations. Those were the only times that white flour was used extensively. On the Christmas loaves of white yeast bread, Mother would lay a twisted piece of dough in the form of an X.

They raised garden stuff, too, in summer. Carrots and cabbages could be stored in the cellar with the potatoes for the daily soups, whose base was meat seasoned with thyme; these were their winter fare. In summer they raised lettuce. They also picked the abundant wild berries—raspberries, strawberries, blueberries, and the delicious red *multer*. These grew low on bushes, making a red carpet in the woods. There was never any attempt to preserve fruits for winter use.

In the latter part of August, when it began to get cold, Father would go with horses and wagon up to the *seter* to bring Mother home. Most horses in Norway were not very big, and those Father owned were buckskin in color. For this shade they were named Skimmerton and Blakken. The wagon would have to be left down on the road, of course, but the horses would be loaded with butter, *gammelost* (old cheese) and *prim* that Mother had made, and then the great procession started. Pack horses led by Father, Mother carrying the baby, chore girls and children driving the herd, calves gamboling alongside and bells ringing—it must have been quite a sight and sound. Down at the road everything that could be was packed into the wagon, and Father helped Mother and the baby up into the seat for the journey home. From there they looked with eager eyes for the roof tops of the Juve place. You can imagine how glad Mother was to see the older children again as they came running to meet her, for our family always held deep affection for each other and enjoyed the mutual company. Big Helga would come bustling out with a wide smile on her face, announcing that she had a hot meal ready and that she hoped the mistress would find everything to her liking. Father and the older children and servants had to hustle the food into the *stabbur*, hardly able to wait for the supper. This *stabbur* was the most important building on the place, because all the food was stored there—grain, meat, and dairy products. The potatoes that had been grown on the farm lowlands would have to be stored in the cellar under the livinghouse to keep them from freezing.

Seterhytte *(mountain cottage)* in Gudbrandsdalen, Norway. Photograph by Darrell Henning.

Stabbur, *Telemark, Norway.* *Photograph by Darrell Henning.*

Two stabbur (storehouses) from Østerdalen at the Norsk Folkemuseum, Oslo, Norway. Photograph by Darrell Henning.

Kviteseid, Telemark. Photograph by Darrell Henning.

Sinnes farm (a private farm), Vradal, Telemark, Norway. Photograph by Darrell Henning.

Glomdals Museum, Elverum, Østerdalen, Norway. Photograph by Darrell Henning.

Farm home, Valdres, Norway. Photograph by Darrell Henning.

Making Bread and Butter

By Thurine Oleson

as told to Erna Oleson Xan

Reprinted from Wisconsin My Home

We had so much company in those early days that Mother had to spend a great deal of her time cooking. She had to be prepared at all times for a visitor, and no one ever went away without a meal or a "treat" of some sort. Though the folks were poor, they still carried on the same hospitable traditions of Norway.

Mother's long blue gingham dress swung back and forth in the cook corner as she began to fix the bread. This white yeast bread was something she had to learn to make in America, but she became so expert at it that her fame spread all over the township. She was a natural-born cook, anyway, and so neat and clean with it that people loved to come there. The bread sponge would be set in the afternoon. This consisted of the potato water left from dinner, and woe to the one who carelessly tossed it out during the dish-washing. Into this water she mashed a few left-over potatoes. Then she put in an old-fashioned dry yeast cake, which had been soaking in lukewarm water. She sprinkled in some salt and sugar, according to the judgment of her practiced hand, and thickened it with flour until it was a little stiffer than pancake batter.

Now this precious sponge in its crock would be wrapped in a clean flour-sack towel, and then in an old white woolen skirt. It would be set on a wooden board on the back of the reservoir to keep warm.

In the evening the big sponge was set. She put lukewarm water in the large brødtraag (bread trough) which Father had hollowed out of a log. This he had scraped with a piece of glass until it shone like glass inside. The bread kept warm longer in a wooden trough than in a metal one, and would rise better. An eight- or ten-loaf batch of bread would take about three quarts of water. To this the sponge was added. With a good stout wooden spoon that Father had also carved for her, she stirred in the flour and gave it all a vigorous beating. Then the clean flour sack, woolen skirt, and pieces of old red blanket were tucked about it, and it was put to bed on a backless chair behind the stove.

In the morning when she opened it, the top was covered with bubbles working as if it were alive. The tingling yeasty odor filled the kitchen. Now she had more sifted flour warmed and ready, which she added with more salt and sugar, and began to knead with all the strength of her stout arms, until the dough was as light as a feather. It must then rise to the top of the trough, when she would tackle it again with might and main. After this last punching it would be bundled into blankets once more, when it would presently fly up to the top of the trough. In the meantime, she had her tins greased with pork-fryings, and as soon as it had risen the second time, she would cut off a piece big enough for a loaf, deftly form it and lay it in the tin. In no time the loaves had swelled to their full capacity, and just as they were about to roll over the sides of the tins, she would put them into the hot oven, where they stayed until they were baked a golden brown. When they came out of the oven, she greased the crust with pork-fryings again, and turned them on edge on a clean breadboard, which had been scrubbed snowy white with sand.

Now all the time it was baking, we children had been getting more and more eager, and our mouths would fairly drip from all the delicious aroma in the kitchen. As soon as one loaf got cool enough, we would begin to beg for a slice. Mother would take up her sharp bread knife and slice into one of the crispy loaves, crumbs flying in brown flakes all over the board. On it she would spread generous slabs of homemade butter, and maybe a slice of *gammelost* (old cheese) and shoo us outside with a pleased smile on her face.

This is how Mother made her butter. When the milk came to the house in pails, she would go with it to the pantry and lift up the ponderous *kjellarlem* (trapdoor), taking it by its big iron ring, and lean the door carefully against the wall. To keep from falling into the hole, she would grasp the shelf above it with her other hand. Then sitting carefully down on the edge of the hole, she sought sure footing on the heavy hand-hewn ladder. Grasping the top rung, she would swish her skirts in after her. Halfway down the ladder, she would stop, and hanging onto a rung, take a long, fearful look around the cellar . . .

After she had made sure that the cellar was safe, she would call to Mathis to lower the pails of milk. These she strained into sweet, scalded shallow milk pans, and set them in shining rows on a long shelf. Now was the time to take the skimmer and skim off the cream from the two-day-old pans. The cream was gathered into a two-gallon crock, and the remaining skim milk poured into the pails for the calves and pigs out in the barn. Then everything would be handed up to the patient waiting Mathis.

The tall stave churn which had been scrubbed and scalded thoroughly and had stood long hours with the hot sun pouring into its mellow golden well, was trundled out from its own corner in the pantry to the warm kitchen. There it was filled with coldest water from the well, to match the temperature of the chilled cream, and the dash handle would stick crazily out of the top. Mother, who seldom had to pump any water, emptied this churn water right out on the ground, and poured her jars of thick gobby cream into the churn in its place. Father now sat in the shade outside, and it was his job to churn rhythmically and steadily until the butter gathered in yellow islands all over the buttermilk. At this he would set up a glad call. *"Thorild, kom, naa har eg smør!"* ("Thorild, come. Now I have butter!") She would come smiling, with a butter ladle and bowl hugged against her round stomach, pleased that the cream had been so nice as to give up its butter so quickly. She also dangled a tin cup in one hand, so that her beloved Mathis might have reward in all the buttermilk he could *orka* (hold).

While he was drinking and smacking his lips, and wiping the white moustache of buttermilk off with the back of his hand, Mother gathered the butter into a lump and put it into her bowl. Over and over again she worked the butter in fresh water until the water finally came off clear. The butter was then salted with old-fashioned barrel salt until her taste said it was enough. Then she packed it into jars, tied a little cloth over the top, and covered it with a plate. After saving out a generous supply for her family, the remaining jars were put in the pantry to be lowered into the cellar. There they awaited the market day, when they would be traded for coffee, flour, sugar, or even clothes at the village store.

Mother's Greatest Fame

By Thurine Oleson

as told to Erna Oleson Xan

Reprinted from Wisconsin My Home

Certain activities took place in the fall of the year, in preparation for the long Wisconsin winter. Mother still had a woman come to make the winter's supply of *flatbrød*. She was a Marta Johnson, who travelled from house to house performing this task. It would take her many days to get enough put by to last till spring.

After they got in a little better circumstances, the folks continued to butcher as much as they had in Norway—four or five small pigs in the fall, a beef, and the lambs in the spring. The best of the pork would be salted down and the remainder made into blood sausage, head cheese, and *sylte* (pickled pigs' feet), liver sausage, and meat sausage made from the scraps, flavored with salt, pepper, and thyme.

When they butchered a beef, the best part would be made into corned beef to eat in the summer. This was done by putting it down in brine in big crocks. In winter the bones were used for soups. These had been salted just a little and kept in the chest in the granary, for they would not be kept over till warm weather. The stew meat was kept in brine, later to be cooked up with potatoes, carrots and onions. As the time went by and the old folks began to lose their teeth, Mother made more and more food that required little chewing. My parents were never sick until their last illnesses at the ages of ninety-three and ninety-five, which attested to the soundness of Mother's feeding and caring for the sturdy bodies they had inherited.

We had soups of all sorts. One of them was a fruit soup which we liked very much. It was made of barley or rice, raisins, prunes and grape juice, sweetened to taste. The grape juice was some she bottled herself every summer. Fruit soup was a supper dish and was eaten with bread and butter, or perhaps with cookies for dessert. A lot of breadstuffs gave heat and energy in that brisk Wisconsin climate.

Mother's greatest fame, however, came from the way she made cheese. You may know that anyone who had gone to a *seter* in Norway from childhood could be counted upon to know her business in that line. She made a wide variety of cheeses and they formed an important part of our diet. I think some kind of cheese was on the table every meal of our lives.

Sweet cheese (*sødost*) was made out of whole sweet milk. Milk was heated on the stove in a copper washboiler to blood warmth, then she added rennet which she had made from calves' stomachs. It was cut in little pieces, put in a muslin bag, and dropped into the milk, causing it to curdle. When the curds were gathered in lumps about the size of one's little finger, she skimmed them out and salted them. Into a clean flour sack they went, then into a vessel to be pressed under the weight of a big, clean stone to remove the whey. It was then put away in a cool place to ripen for a few weeks, when it was considered ready. Off would come the sack, and the round cheese, now firm and of smooth texture, would delight the eye and cause the mouth to water in anticipation. A triangle would be cut out of this smooth cheese to be sliced at table. How good it was, laid on top of Mother's delicious bread and butter! When this *sødost* got old and hard, Mother cut it in chunks and put it in brine, when it would turn green and yellow in places. This was the time that Ole Stromme, an old neighbor, would say,

> *Ja naar osten blir saa gammel*
> *At den er gul og grøn,*
> *Da er den god!*
> (When the cheese is so old
> That it is green and gold,
> Then it is good!)

This green and gold cheese could be kept all winter in the big wooden food chest in the granary.

The whey from this sweet cheese was put into the big copper kettle and hung on a strong pole laid on the old-fashioned fireplace out in back of the cook shanty. Father had made this fireplace of field stone and mortar, and it was known as the "*eisa.*" It was circular, about thirty inches high, with a place cut out in front to put the wood in. The whey in this copper kettle was cooked all day, and it had to be stirred many hours with a *sleiv*, a great, long, wooden spoon with a flat bowl about five inches wide, which Father had made. It was Father's job to stir the whey to keep it from sticking to the bottom of the kettle, and to keep the fire going with fat tamarack chips and stout oak chunks. When the *prim* (whey cheese) was cooked down about as thick as apple butter, the fire was allowed to die down, but still the mixture had to be stirred until it got cold. One had to stand up to do this stirring. Father would be relieved now and then by Mother, or one of the children, who took to the task with unwilling hearts, but we never dared to demur, for Mother's tongue was as sharp as a splinter. After the *prim* was cold, it was put in crocks, sealed with melted butter, and a clean rag tied around the top, then more paper to keep it clean. An old plate was put on top of the paper to keep out the mice, who were as fond of Mother's cheese as we were.

When the time came for the *prim* to be used, it was dished out with a strong spoon, enough for a meal at a time. If one didn't like it dry, it could be boiled up with a little water and sugar and restored to freshness. Or it did not need to ripen at all, but could be spooned out of the crock and mixed with cream and sugar, and spread on bread and butter. This way it was a summer spread. If it was to be saved for winter, it was cooked somewhat longer, and shaped into dry hard balls, and laid in a dry place.

But chief of all the cheeses was *gammelost* (old cheese). Any Norwegian, near or far, will smack his lips and take a deep breath at the sound of the memorable word.

The first step in making *gammelost* was to make cottage cheese out of clabbered sour milk. It was put at the back of the cook stove in an iron kettle and allowed to stand with a few stirrings, until the curds rose to the top in in a smooth mass. This was skimmed off and put into a clean cloth, and hung up on a hook over a table, with a pan set under to catch the whey. The whey from *gammelost* was too small and sour a portion for *prim*, for which the pigs in the barnyard were very glad. They would stand with their front feet in the trough and squeal at the top of their voices when they smelled it coming.

Now you could stop here and have cottage cheese for supper, by mixing the curds with salt and cream. However, if you wanted *gammelost*, it was first hung longer, so as to get it very dry. Then it was crumbled fine between the hands and put into a stone pan, a hole scooped in the middle of it and the cheese pushed to the side of the pan. A clean cloth was put over it, and then it was let to stand in a warm place, sprinkled with water every day until it began to "work" and smell rotten. Then the cloth was removed and a little water poured on it. Caraway seed and salt were added to taste, and you could eat it right away on bread and butter, when Norwegian noses, tongues, and hearts were most satisfied. Or you could put it away in a covered jar, for the longer it stood, the more *gammel* (old) it got, and the more tantalizing to the nose, which had so much to do with the enjoyment of this delicacy. When it ran together in a greyish, flecked mass and smelled strong enough to knock you back down the cellar steps, it attained the height of the genuine and highly-prized *appetitost* (appetite cheese). More could not be expected of food on earth. Then it was almost revered, as was due its age and excellence.

Another way to fix *gammelost* before it got too old, was to put it in a pan and boil it with a little milk and caraway seed, when it would turn a glossy grey. It was poured in a jar to cool, whence it could be cut in nice shiny slices. *Gammelost* was too powerful to keep. The worms found out about it after just so long a time. So it was made frequently both summer and winter. . . .

Desserts were not much in use at our house. We got our sweets from a little rock candy which was kept up in the screen cupboard and dispensed for good behavior. In summer and fall Mother prepared apple sauce by cutting the fruit, removing the blossom end and stewing it with sugar and a little water. After many years in this new country, the women began to do a little canning. They learned to make different kinds of pickles, which added a tart flavor to our winter meals. Mother's favorites were green tomato pickles, sweet ripe cucumber pickles, and chow-chow. She used to make gallons of that, and put it down in stone jars. Sweet crab-apple pickles were a treat, too, and crab-apple jelly and plum jelly. As the years went on and the apple orchard that brother Ole set out began to bear, there was plenty of apple-sauce to liven up the winter fare.

People appreciated Mother's cooking, and never failed to tell her so. Our neighbor, Ole Stromme, when he rose from a meal at our house, never forgot to say, "This was the best meal I ever ate in my living time." To which Mother, bursting with pride, would rock her head from side to side and reply modestly, *"Aa nei, det var ikkje so svært."* (Oh, no, that was not so great.) But she could not conceal a very pleased look on her face. She might not have been able to bring with her the riches that were hers in Norway to this raw new land, but she could bring her skill and her open hands and heart. These no one could take away from her, no matter where she went.

All the time her adoring Mathis would look up at her with a loving smile and nod his head to agree with Mr. Stromme, saying, *"Ja ja ja. Det var godt, Thorild."* (Yes, indeed, it was good, Thorild.)

Our house was not too unusual in respect to cleanliness and hospitality, although I believe Mother was the best cook in the neighborhood. Everybody kept a neat house, and bounteous meals could be set before company at short notice.

One exception to this rule was Anne and Torger's youngest daughter, Maria. Anne had been so fond of her that she had spoiled her. When Maria married, she had children so fast that she did nothing but tend to them, and they were so fat and pretty that it was a sight to see. But she couldn't be bothered about the house.

When you came to see Maria, her arms reached out in the heartiest welcome, and there was not the slightest embarrassment on her part if the house was in a mess. She would be so glad to see you that she would hasten to clear out a chair and dust it with her apron, and then you must sit right down and tell her all the news, while she would tell you hers.

There wouldn't be a thing to eat in the house, but that didn't bother Maria a bit. While she visited with you, she got out her stave churn, poured in some cream, and set it beside her chair. As the dasher went up and down, it kept time with her cozy chatter. Pretty soon she would have butter, and would work up a generous pat for the table. With the buttermilk she would make the most delicious soda biscuits you ever tasted in your life. These she would set on the table by the butter pat, and set on a dish of elegant tomato or plum preserves. With these went cups of steaming hot coffee, floating with thick cream. Visitors somehow went away from Maria's house feeling that they had had a kingly meal.

Meats, Potatoes, Berries and Nuts

By Thurine Oleson

as told to Erna Oleson Xan

Reprinted from Wisconsin My Home

A little way from the house stood a small building we called the cook shanty. It had just three walls and a slanting roof; the front was all open. Inside were an old cook stove and a long bench to set ourselves and the waterpail on. A few shelves along the back part of it held the pans and kettles. There was just an earthen floor which we kept swept clean with a broom. Oh dear, how many good meals my mother cooked in that shanty! The new potatoes and sweet corn! Good salt pork was about the only kind of meat we had through the summer, and we never got tired of it fried, with milk gravy made from the drippings. I could never tire of eating the crispy meat, and chewing the brittle browned rind. Often we had corned beef. On Sunday we would have chicken sometimes, with lots of gravy and fluffy yellow dumplings.

By fall the salt pork would be used up, too, and then we would kill a sheep or two. We had smoked hams and bacon once in a while, but not until we were older. The farmers seemed to prefer the salted meat in those early days. . . .

My father, whose job it was to scrub the new potatoes for Mother, fixed up some sort of brush to skin them, and it would not be hard for anyone to do the same today. It was made as they had made them in Norway, of a lot of twigs from a certain stout bush, which were tied securely around a broom handle, and the brush cut off even. The potatoes were put in a pail and covered with water and then stomped with the brush until the skins were all off. When he would pour this water off and rinse the potatoes, they were smooth and shining, ready to cook. I can see my father now, stomping those potatoes, outside the little cook shanty. Father always brought in the vegetables and killed the chickens. He loved my mother so that it was a pleasure to help her in any way.

In those days the only tame berries we had were currants, but there were all kinds of wild red raspberries and blackcaps and blackberries and strawberries. We found them along fences. At the end of our farm was a marsh, and along the south side of it, where the land was low, there were masses of these bushes. The pails of raspberries I picked there I could not remember now, but I know there were a good many of them each season. On the other side of this marsh were strawberries. Wild strawberries were not so very big, but so sweet and good. . . .

Hazelnut bushes grew thick along the zig-zag rail fences and all over the woods on that long hill on our farm. . . . We would haul these hazelnuts home and lay them on top of the roof of the cook shanty. It was so low on the back end that we could easily get up there by standing on a barrel or something. We emptied our bags of hazelnuts on the roof and let them lie there in the sun until they were dry enough to shuck. Then, how we cracked and ate them! We used to find a stone that had a little hollow place, and lay them in there and crack them with a hammer.

Then came hickory-nut time. Picking was my job, if we had to climb the trees to get them. There were hickory trees all over the farm. There was one great, tall tree on the side of the big hill whose branches were high from the ground. But the nuts were as large as small crab apples, and if we did not get them the squirrels would. When I got old enough to worry about it, I stood under that tree one day and looked longingly at those big nuts, wondering how in the world I could get at them. They were even too high from the ground to reach with a long stick. So I said to myself, I am going to see if I can climb that tree. I took a long stick in one hand (it seems impossible now) and grasped the trunk with both hands, hitching myself up that tree like a monkey, and finally reached the lowest branch. From then on it was easy, for I could climb from branch to branch and hit the nuts off with the long stick. I tell you I was proud to be the first person to conquer that tree, but the nuts were worth it. If I had not been born with that determination and strength, I guess I would have been dead long ago. My lifetime motto has been, "Never get stuck."

These nuts would have been eaten up by our big family quicker than the squirrels had it not been for quick-thinking brother John. He laid them on boards across the upstairs rafters in the house, where they had a fine place to dry. A few at a time would be brought down and put in a round tin box which was kept under the kitchen lounge. Very nice cakes would be decorated or filled with these delicious nut meats, and many were the long evenings when the wind and snow were whirling outside, that we children sat on the couch and cracked and ate the good nuts.

There were many wild grape vines around the farm, too, in those days. We children had to go after the grapes with baskets, and we had to be careful not to crush them. My mother made wine, as was the style everywhere, and treated the friends who came to see us. This is what the grapes were used for. Sometimes she made wine out of currants. That was really delicious.

Baking for Weddings

By Thurine Oleson

as told to Erna Oleson Xan

Reprinted from Wisconsin My Home

By the time I was seventeen, I was a pretty good baker and cook, and had the honor of being asked to bake at two weddings. The first one was for our Irish neighbors, the Nesbitts. Jim was getting married. His bride was from New London, Wisconsin, about forty miles away. Ella was a cozy, rosy-cheeked, brown-eyed, darkhaired Irish girl. She wore a red worsted dress that evening and was very pretty, and they were very much in love. There had already been a Catholic wedding in her home town, so this was just the celebration at his home. I baked quite a few cakes, though, light ones and dark ones. His mother, Maggie, made some very good bread, and as the custom was in those days, there were always nice raised biscuits, made like bread except that we added sugar and shortening and sometimes dried currants. As I remember they had roast turkey and all that went with it, and tea, as the Irish very seldom drank coffee. Not the Nesbitts, anyway. . . .

The other wedding where I was head baker was at my cousin Lena Johnson's, where the young folks used to gather and have so good a time on Sunday afternoons. This was a very big wedding. The couple was married in the church in the afternoon, and after that came to her home for the big wedding dinner and celebration.

It took us two or three days to bake enough cakes for this affair. Another girl helped me, but she said she would not take the blame if things went wrong, so it was up to me to go ahead. Oh, of all the cakes at this wedding! I guess they expected seventy or eighty people. We made white cakes, dark cakes, silver and gold cakes, chocolate and coconut cakes, maybe a couple of each kind. Layers and loaf cakes, too. The wedding cake was a three-tiered fruit cake, filled with all kinds of raisins and currants and maybe citron. The bottom was made in a good-sized, round milkpan, the next a little smaller pan, and the top the smallest of all. It was a pretty, white-frosted cake, and good tasting. We had everything we wanted to do with, plenty of eggs, cream, butter, and milk in those days, for you could not get much for anything at the store, so we did not have to spare the ingredients. Then there was lovely bread and those good sweet raised biscuits with currants, shortening, and sugar in them. Halvor had butchered a calf for meat, and they had mashed potatoes, pickles of all kinds, and jelly; mince and apple pies, and coffee made in the washboiler. There was not another inch to spare on the tables for all the food. Luckily I was not responsible for all this food, just the cakes and cookies. And don't think any of us got paid for it. It was supposed to be a great honor, and it was. You had to have people you could trust and who knew their business when you had such an important event as a wedding.

We Didn't Drink Milk

By Thurine Oleson
as told to Erna Oleson Xan
Reprinted from Wisconsin My Home

At Sunday breakfast, Father would first have one of Mother's good cups of Peaberry coffee, made rich golden tan with lumps of cream. Next he would reach for one of her thick slices of bread and cut it in lengthwise strips, then crosswise, making cubes. Upon each of these he would lay delicious yellow butter, almost as thick as the bread, and eat each cube with a smack of his lips. We children couldn't wait to go to all this trouble, but bit hungrily from the big slices. We would all enjoy the sausage and *prim* and crisp sugar cookies, and of course, the grownups would have cup after cup of hot coffee. We children drank water. With all that milk around, you would have thought they would have fed us that, but it never seemed to occur to them. We just didn't drink sweet milk as a beverage, but we had plenty of it with *grøt*, in cooked food, in cheese, and as clabber.

Kaffe (Coffee)

Coffee was little used in Europe before the 1700's and it did not become common in most rural areas in Norway until almost a century later. Since it was imported, it remained scarce and expensive through the period of mass emigration in the 19th century. Few immigrants would have known coffee as an everyday drink before they came to America, where it was plentiful and moderate in price.

Teakettles, first made for the open fire and then altered to fit the opening on a stove, are products of the coffee and tea culture. So are cups and saucers, creamers and sugars and coffee and tea pots. Most of these were imported until Norway began its first large ceramic factories in the late 19th century. Sugar cutters for chopping lumps from the larger blocks are also products of the coffee culture.

Coffee was originally sold as green beans which had to be roasted in a long-handled pan resembling a corn popper. In the 1700's the beans were ground with a wood mortar and pestle or crushed with a wood roller in a trough. In the 19th century these primitive instruments gradually gave way to grinders with metal burrs hand-turned with a crank.

Vesterheim,

The Norwegian-American Museum,

Decorah, Iowa

The Old Ironstone Platter

Erna Oleson Xan

Reprinted with permission of *The Birmingham News*, Birmingham, Alabama.

Mama loved a bargain. She had to be a sharp shopper, for there was a house to furnish and a flock of children to feed. We never forgot the day she happened upon a sale of household goods, where she found a huge white ironstone platter.

It was warped a little, but this defect was offset by a blue trademark on the bottom with a recumbent greyhound encircled in laurel, and beneath it, "T. & R. Boote, Royal Premium, Ironstone."

"English," she said to herself, and hefted it.

Mama knew well the clatter of china. She would always close her eyes and wince before she looked to see what the children had broken. Naturally, she loved the platter instantly.

"They'll never break this," she said. "They'll never be able to lift it till they're grown."

Costing but 50 cents, second-hand and twisted, let no one think that this platter was used "for common." It went on the high pantry shelf, where it lay upside down in majestic solitude.

"Your mother is a wonderful woman," Papa said, proud of her thrift and management.

It was like money in the bank. Mama knew that whenever company came, whenever there was a holiday like Thanksgiving, she had the platter to suit the occasion. It was always filled: chicken and dumplings; boiled dinner with ham-hock, cabbage, potatoes and carrots; in butchering time, fried pork, or stacks of baked ribs and sauerkraut; or beef roasted slowly, so that it was crusty brown outside and fork-tender within, the platter was always the center of festivities.

It made us feel rich, and Papa's face beamed as he watched Mama bear it and its steaming contents to the table.

Living in the country as we did, the children had to leave home in their teens to go to school. Thanksgiving was the first real holiday that brought us all home, and each wondered what Mama would have for the great day.

We were very fond of roast goose. Mama kept a flock for their meat and feathers, but geese were hissy and hateful. To be sure, they stayed at home, unlike the turkeys that stole away and had to be hunted over half the township. Turkeys were foolish, but geese were mean. One time a gander overturned our terrier, trod on his stomach and pecked him in the face. The gander had to be beaten off with a broom.

A platter of glazed brown stuffed goose was welcomed with cheers.

Chickens had to be selected more carefully. Chickens were pets, would ride on one's shoulder, and lay eggs under the back stoop as a special favor. "This isn't Blackie?" we asked, when chicken and dressing was heaped on the ironstone platter. Mama smiled comfortingly and said "No."

The table had been stretched to full length, laid with white linen, centered with a fluted glass bowl full of fruit. There was a long crystal celery dish; tri-cornered glass hat of jelly; pickles; a smooth pat of butter; and a pyramid of Mama's feather-light "Winter Luck" rolls.

107

Then came the ironstone platter. Prayer was said, plates were heaped, and the table was encircled with happy faces at the joy of being together once more.

When we came home for Thanksgiving, we often found an extra person on hand. Once it was Sam, a little Italian who had attached himself to our home. The harvest was in, but the homeless wanderer begged to work for his room and board. Papa let him shovel snow, help with the milking, and Sam went around the neighborhood doing day work.

For the young ladies' home-coming, Sam "washed up good." For Thanksgiving dinner he put on his best coat, shirt, red tie and "highwater" pants. He crossed himself quickly after the prayer, and a wide grin split his swarthy face when he saw Mama coming with the platter.

After dinner, he motioned me into the parlor. Sam had met a girl. I must write a letter for him, saying he had bought her a "ruby ring."

"But you don't send rings unless you are engaged," I protested.

"In my cahntree," he insisted, "we send 'em a r-ring." I did not know where to put my face while he dictated his amorous note.

Another time when we came home, the extra person was an old Indian from the reservation, who was cutting wood for Papa. Faithful, well-mannered, intelligent, Alec came and went in our home for years. With a slight nod of thanks when invited to table, or a smouldering twinkle in his black eyes at our chatter, Alec mostly applied himself with knife and fork to his generous plate.

Grandma and Grandpa often came for Thanksgiving, if the snow wasn't too deep for the little brass-banded Ford. Sometimes the folks from Canada came. Strangers or cherished relatives—all were welcomed around the table.

The old home has been sold now, and the old folks have passed away. But the 50-cent bargain, the English ironstone platter, still warped, still unchipped, is mine. I get it out when the children come, and heap it high with good things, as in the days of long ago.

Child Helpers

Even then Mama always organized a kitchen "fly-chasing" after the noon dinner. Each child was handed a half-broom-stick with long strips of newspaper or sacks tacked onto the end. They made a noise like rustling dry leaves when shaken.

Window shades were pulled down. The door closest to the sun was left open, and the rest of the room was dark. A child was stationed in each corner with her "fly-chaser" which she was supposed to keep shaking softly, so as not to scare the flies, but just to keep them from alighting on anything.

At Mama's command, all children began to move slowly toward the door, shaking their noise-makers, and when all the flies converged there in the light, she opened the door quickly and shooed them hastily out, and slammed the door shut.

Of course, by supper-time they were all back, clinging to the outside of the screen, which in the meantime had been fly-sprayed (and they just loved it) and were waiting to sneak in as the men came for supper.   E.O.X.

The Pie Safe

Remember the old double-doored "pie-safe" that stood in the corner of the kitchen? Head high, its sides and doors were of wire screening, or sheets of thin tin with fancy patterns pierced into them by small nails and slight taps of the hammer.

Pies, cakes, cookies, bread, and leftovers from the noon dinner were all kept there, safe from flies. Oil lamps were kept on top for safety's sake in the daytime. These safes were also mouse-proof. *E.O.X.*

Pets

Remember when the dog ate table-scraps off a battered pie-tin on the back porch, instead of raw ground beef from a white, sterile, store-bought bowl on a waxed kitchen floor?

Remember when the cat ate mice instead of $3.00-a-bag "Minnie-Meouw?" *E.O.X.*

The Sacks

Remember when your Papa brought home a 50-lb. bag of white cane sugar for canning time, and you would use almost all of it "putting things up" for winter? Every now and then, he also came home with a 100-lb. sack of white flour on his shoulder.

Sugar sacks were of cheaper cotton that shrank and wrinkled in the wash, and were often cut crooked to begin with. But they were good enough, after much scrubbing and boiling, to be hemmed up on the sewing machine and used for dish-towels.

The flour sacks were a different matter. They were of such good cotton material that they could be hemmed by hand, embroidered with a red strawberry and green leaves, or a rose, initialed, and given as gifts, particularly at bridal showers. They didn't leave lint on newly washed water-glasses.

Everyday pillow-cases were made out of flour sacks, and four or more sacks could be sewn together to make summer bed-sheets.

Until country kids went to high school, their everyday panties and petticoats were made of boiled and bleached flour sacks, as were the little girls' "Ferris Waists." This was a sort of light, sleeveless jacket, worn underneath a slip, with buttons to hold up the panties, and fasteners to attach long garters which held up the long black or white stockings.

Of course, there was always the matter of getting the red, green, or blue brand-names out of the material. Soaked in cold water first, then scrubbed in lye and strong brown soap (no rubber gloves in those days, dearie), then boiled in the copper boiler on the stove. That's what it took to transform a sugar or flour sack into household material.

Even then, once in a while, a child might bend over too far, and there, before all eyes, one could decipher across the little bottom, the faint but legible letters that said, "Mother's Best." *E.O.X.*

Going Nutting

On Saturday afternoons in the fall, you took a gunny sack or basket and went nutting. Along the fence rows, the hazelnuts were bursting out of their frilly burrs.

The black walnuts' crinkly shells stained your fingers as if you had been smoking "coffin nails," but oh, how good those nuts tasted in cookies.

The paper-shell hickory nuts you could knock down with a long stick. Who can forget Mama's real-butter three-layered cakes, frosted with inch-high real-butter icing, the top laid solid all over from edge to edge in ever-narrowing circles with those golden hickory nut meat halves? *E.O.X.*

Mosquito Netting

Remember when mosquitoes and flies were kept out of the house, not by screens, but by mosquito netting that was a stiff black or white big-meshed cheese cloth? Mama would tack them up at every lower-window frame each spring. Real screen-wire was affordable only for screen doors. *E.O.X.*

Norwegian Manners

When you went to visit *Bestemor* (grandmother), after the meal, everyone got up and stood at the back of his or her chair, placed hands on the top of the chair, bowed to her, and said, *"Takk for maten."* (Thanks for the food.)

When the polite old Norwegian pioneers met, they would shake hands heartily, and in a most cordial voice would say, *"Takk for sist!"* (Thanks for the last time we met.)

In the pioneer Norwegian-American homes, invitations to a wedding were issued verbally, as in the Old Country, by a man going the rounds on horseback. One time, Erna's mother, Thurine, remembered that a man came by *on foot. Bestemor* Thorhild could not get over such a flagrant breach of etiquette. But the family attended the wedding anyway, so as not to hurt the feelings of the bride's parents.

In the old Norwegian-American homes, it was not considered nice for a woman to speak or express an opinion when the minister was a guest at a meal. But one time, the minister was so taken with the boiled potatoes that he asked, "How do you get them so *mealy*?"

Nobody was bold enough to answer, of course, except a pert young married woman, waiting on table, who spoke up and said, "*Shake* them, and *then* they'll be mealy!" (It became a 'potato joke' that has never died down to this day.)

When anyone invited for a meal could not come, Erna's mother, Thurine Oleson, would quote an old Norwegian saying, *"Tilbud's mat er så godt som spist"* (Bidden food is as good as eaten.) In other words, the honor is in the asking. *E.O.X.*

The Norway Building at Little Norway, Blue Mounds, Wisconsin. With dragon heads at the peaks of the gables, this charming building is a reproduction of a 12th-century stavkirke (Norwegian church). It was assembled with peg construction in Trondheim, Norway, then disassembled and shipped in pieces to the Columbian Exposition of 1893, in Chicago. The building was donated to Little Norway in 1935 by Phillip Wrigley. The building is open to the public May 1 through the last Sunday in October. Blue Mounds is adjacent to Mt. Horeb, 25 miles west of Madison, Wisconsin. Photograph courtesy of Little Norway.

The other stavkirke *in America is the Chapel in the Hills at Rapid City, South Dakota. It is the exact copy of a stave church built 800 years ago at Borgund, Norway. Visitors may attend the Vesper services conducted every evening in the summer. This stave church was the home of the Lutheran Vespers Radio Program.*

Photograph courtesy of Chapel in the Hills.

The Aprons of Vesterheim

The collections of Vesterheim, the Norwegian-American Museum at Decorah, Iowa, are enriched by 122 examples of the use of aprons as a folk art medium.

The aprons were created by Evelina Marie Oppegard Grimes (1900-1983) of Minneapolis, Minnesota. Her stitchwork succeeds in conveying the richness of human life and aspiration, as well as the entertaining virtues of whimsy and poetry.

At Vesterheim, the aprons have been arranged in thematic groupings illustrating biblical themes, the seasons, the cycle of life, farm life, holidays, religion, current events, travel, teenagers, and romance. They are laced with poignancy, folk wisdom, and nostalgia. The aprons are not of the type used with the Norwegian national costume, but the small American apron used by hostesses when serving guests.

For a series that Mrs. Grimes called "From the Beginning Until Now," the first apron was of Eve. It is bright green with embroidered leaves and two red apples for pockets. Her Minnesota apron depicts blue sky, forests of green, a moccasin, and a loon—the state bird. One apron depicts the skyline of New York City. Another shows all roads leading to a Dairy Queen drive-in.

For a Leif Erickson day celebration, Mrs. Grimes stitched a Viking ship of the type he would have sailed on his 1000 A. D. voyage of discovery to the New World.

The farm aprons are especially delightful. They depict cattle, a figure walking toward the gate on a snowy night, grandma's old-fashioned country kitchen, grandma's dining room with its preciously filled plate rail, grandma's garden, the barnyard, and a little white country church.

Evelina knew farm life well. Born near Faribault, Minnesota, she and five other children grew up on what Evelina called "a rockbound farm." The father died while the children were small, and the mother brought up the children alone.

Evelina was Norwegian-American. Her husband Gordon, who worked for General Mills, was of English heritage. Evelina and her husband had three sons and a daughter: Rodney, an attorney in Minneapolis; Richard, a machinist with mechanical inclinations like his father; Vernon, a mechanical engineer; and Shirley Dickey, a secretary.

Evelina and Gordon traveled many miles to present her show "Travelogue with Evelina's Originals," featuring her poetry and her aprons. Retiring from this career in 1975 because of failing health, she asked her friend Mrs. Ione N. (Brack) Kadden to take over the programs. Mrs. Kadden accepted and gave many presentations in the next 13 years.

Poetry of The Aprons

In little old log cabins and in humble homes of yore
Many were the uses of the apron Grandma wore.
For fancy holders, Grandma never gave a second thought,
She simply used her apron to move a pan or pot.
In replenishing her wood box as every housewife should,
She used her apron to carry chips and kindling wood.
When her garden yielded harvests, to swell their humble means
Aprons full she gathered of carrots, peas, and beans.
Should summer rain clouds threaten to send a sudden squall
Her baby chicks she gathered, and when she found them all,
They nestled in her apron and were carried to the shed,
The old hen clucking right behind, to a safe warm bed.
Her apron was a signal as she waved it in the air
To Grandpa in the field to partake of humble fare.
In exasperation she shooed the flies from the kitchen door,
Or the chickens after feeding when they squawked for more.
Perhaps the night was chilly when she made a friendly call;
Then she tucked the apron on her shoulders if she forgot her paisley shawl.
If caught out in a sudden shower it some protection lent,
Although my Grandma never had a Toni permanent!
At times behind its ample folds a timid child might hide,
Babies also slept beneath it on a long and tiresome ride.
Often there were times when a little one was hurt at play,
Then with the corner of her apron, Grandma wiped the tears away.
And when at last, it was worn, torn, and patched beyond repair,
She found further use for it; to waste. . .she did not dare.
Its threadbare lengths were cut in squares, for little runny noses
Or for scratched-up knees or little busted toeses,
Or perhaps in company with Grandpa's shirt and overalls
It ended in a carpet that stretched to all four walls.
If aprons could but speak, they would have stories by the score
For many were the uses of the apron Grandma wore.
Yes, many were the uses of the apron Grandma wore,
But today there are aprons for each and every chore:
For company, my lady wears a frilly, fussy one,
But one a lot more sturdy, when gardening must be done.
And in the kitchen a special one, when baking cakes or pies or beans,
But more often you will find her in her faded, skin-tight *jeans!*

—*Evelina Marie Grimes*

From, *Wisps of Whimsy and Touches of Truth*. . .published 1978

I Never Sew on Sunday

To My Mother
By Evelina Marie Grimes

"Six days thou shalt labor; the seventh thou shalt rest.
"Thus the Lord commanded His people whom he blest.
This law my mother lived by; the children learned the rule
That Sunday was for worship, and then for Bible school.
Of course there were exceptions; the cattle must be fed,
We cared for the disabled, who were confined to bed.
Our Sunday best was set in order on the night before,
With handmade laces gracing the petticoats we wore.
On Sunday morning was no time for late repair,
For should a strategic button be hanging by one thread,
Mother calmly told me, "Use a safety pin instead."
Though modesty was thus preserved, this I must confess,
I still can feel that telltale pin showing through my dress.
Yes, many times I'm tempted, because my Sunday's free,
A hem line just to alter as fashion might decree.
But I never sew on Sunday, though many good folks do;
It is a torch I carry, Mother dear, for you.

From, *Wisps of Whimsy and Touches of Truth*. . .published 1978

Discovery of America

By Evelina Grimes

115

The Way to the Dairy Queen

New York

Man on the Moon

By Evelina Grimes

116

Embroidery
By Grace Rikansrud

The meticulous embroideries of Grace Rikansrud of Decorah, Iowa were included in the exhibition from Vester-heim, NORWAY IN AMERICA, at Hamar, Lillehammer, and Gjøvik, Norway in 1989.

Below: Table runner with black pattern-darned embroidery, 1980s.
Bottom: Embroidered cuff of Voss type.
Top right: Table runner with pulled work.
Middle right: Doily with Hardanger embroidery.

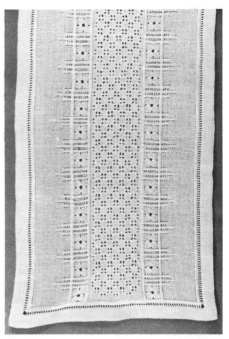

Jewelry in the Vesterheim Collection

Masterpieces of filagree decoration (gold or silver wires or beads soldered to a flat surface or formed into open work) are found in Scandinavia from shortly after the time of Christ. The work may not have a continuous history, but it was popular in the rural areas of Norway, primarily for jewelry but also for spoon handles, small boxes, and the like, in the late 18th and 19th centuries. Elaborate pieces of the type shown here generally date from after 1850.

Concave spangles with thin gold plating often cover the surface of filagree brooches ("søljer"). This type is called a rose brooch with spangles. It is found in Norway's central valleys from Setesdal in the south to Hallingdal farther north. The brooches had a central position on the woman's bunad.

Heart and crown brooches are more common in Sweden than in Norway, but this filagree type often appears in Norway's eastern valleys.

Below: Needle cases in the form of fish were not common. This example is from the late 1700s. The head folds back to open the case.

1896 Photographs
of Norway

Wilh. Dreesen, Hof-fotograf i Flensburg

Torghatten.

Svolvær (Lofoten).

Merok (Geirangerfjord).

Bergen (Fisketorvet).

Lerfosen ved Trondhjem.

Næröfjorden ved Gudvangen.

Nærödalen med Stalheims Hotel.

Odde (Hardanger).

Lotefos (Hardanger).

Lappeleir.

Skorö (Hvalfangerstation).

*The Dayton House, a Norwegian cafe, is next door to Vesterheim,
the Norwegian-American Museum at Decorah, Iowa.*

More Books by Mail

Prices include postage and handling to one address; 1990 prices subject to change. Iowans add 4% sales tax.

Time-Honored Norwegian Recipes Adapted to the American Kitchen This book by mail: $12.95; 2 for $24; 3 for $32.

Wisconsin My Home The story of Thurine Oleson by her daughter Erna Oleson Xan. 224 pages. Perfect-bound, $12.

You may mix the next five titles for special prices: One book $7.95; 2 for $15; 3 for $18.

Notably Norwegian: Recipes, Festivals, Folk Arts 88 pages, 24 in color, highlight Norwegian-American heritage.

Superbly Swedish: Recipes and Traditions 88 pages, 16 in color, includes wonderful food and costumes.

Delectably Danish: Recipes and Reflections 64 pages, 16 in color, recipes of the food Danes are famous for.

Delightfully Dutch: Recipes and Traditions 88 pages, 16 in color; celebrates the Dutch in America.

The Czech Book: Recipes and Traditions 60 pages include color photos, over 120 recipes, and delightful stories of Czechoslovak-Americans.

Scandinavian Christmas, 5 1/2x8 1/2 inches, 40 pages, $6; 2 for $10; 3 for $14.
Scandinavian Proverbs, 5 1/2x8 1/2 inches, 101 sayings, all in beautiful calligraphy, $7.95
Nils Discovers America: Adventures with Erik, by Julie McDonald. Norse mythology in a contemporary setting. Ages 6-11. 5 1/2x8 1/2 inches, 120 pages. $9.95

Stocking Stuffers. Recipe-card-file size. 1 book $5.95; 2 for $10; 3 for $13.50, 4 for $16:

Intriguing Italian Recipes
Pleasing Polish Recipes
Norwegian Recipes
Fine Finnish Foods
Splendid Swedish Recipes
Dear Danish Recipes
Great German Recipes
Cherished Czech Recipes
My Book: Rosemaled cover, blank pages.

Scandinavian Holiday Recipes
A Taste for Health: Low-fat,
  Low-cholesterol Recipes
Fantastic Oatmeal Recipes
Microwave Recipes
Desserts
License to Cook New Mexico Style
Marvelous Minnesota Recipes
Recipes from the Hawkeye State
(Iowa)

Penfield Press
215 Brown Street
Iowa City, Iowa 52245